SACRED MOTIVES

10 REASONS

TO *WAKE* UP *TOMORROW*

AND LIVE FOR *GOD*

PAUL W. CHAPPELL

First published in 2012 by Striving Together Publications, a ministry of Lancaster Baptist Church, Lancaster, CA 93535. Striving Together Publications is committed to providing tried, trusted, and proven books that will further equip local churches to carry out the Great Commission. Your comments and suggestions are valued.

Striving Together Publications
4020 E. Lancaster Blvd.
Lancaster, CA 93535
800.201.7748

Cover design by Andrew Jones
Layout by Craig Parker
Edited by Cary Schmidt and Monica Bass
Special thanks to our proofreaders

The author and publication team have put forth every effort to give proper credit to quotes and thoughts that are not original with the author. It is not our intent to claim originality with any quote or thought that could not readily be tied to an original source.

ISBN 978-1-59894-199-9
Printed in the United States of America

DEDICATION

To Cary Schmidt—

A faithful servant of Christ

A helper and friend in ministry

A co-laborer with sacred motives

CONTENTS

INTRODUCTION   VII

CHAPTER ONE—**The Glory of God**   1

CHAPTER TWO—**A Lost World**   11

CHAPTER THREE—**My Acceptance in Christ**   23

CHAPTER FOUR—**The Word of God**   35

CHAPTER FIVE—**The Love of Christ**   45

CHAPTER SIX—**The Local Church**   55

CHAPTER SEVEN—**The Generations Following Me**   67

CHAPTER EIGHT—**My Family**   81

CHAPTER NINE—**My Country's Need for Revival**   95

CHAPTER TEN—**My Calling in Christ**   109

CONCLUSION   121

INTRODUCTION

"It doesn't matter why you do it…just do your duty!" The voice was loud and forceful, and the speaker was stressing this point. "God doesn't care why you do what you do…motives don't matter! He only cares if you do it!"

I was sitting in a preaching service. I knew the preacher was well intentioned, but something about this point of the message really struck me. Does the Christian life and ministry really boil down to this proposition?

"Motives are irrelevant. Just do your duty."

Duty sounds solid. The concept of doing what is right just because it is right rings true. But is it true that motives are irrelevant—that God doesn't care "why" we do what we do? Does it all boil down to behavior? Or is God also concerned about what drives our behavior?

And digging deeper, if motives matter, in what way do they matter? Are there some motives that please God more than others? And when we give account before Him, will He reckon both "what" we did, and "why" we did it? If so, will some motives be more pleasing to Him than others?

I have heard plenty of well-intentioned and good men of God teach that motives don't really matter. They argue that what we do is more important than why we do it. On one hand, I'm thankful for every work for God that is accomplished, regardless of the motive behind it. Like the Apostle Paul, I praise God whenever Christ is magnified and His name is proclaimed—whether it is done "in pretence, or in truth" (Philippians 1:18).

Yet, I believe the Bible is clear that our motives in the Christian life and ministry matter. In fact, they matter a lot. God desires that we, the servants of Christ, would do "the will of God from the heart" (Ephesians 6:6). God cares about our hearts. From God's perspective, the heart is the focal point—the source of all pure and genuine ministry. He looks on the heart. He examines the heart. He cares passionately about whether the heart is close to Him or far from Him. In fact, several times in His Word He declares that ministry and worship may as well be "put away" when it comes from a heart that is far from Him.

In Isaiah 29:13, God plainly differentiates between the outward motions or words of worship and the heart or motives behind the worship: "Wherefore the Lord said, Forasmuch as this people draw near me with their mouth, and with their lips do honour me, but have removed their heart far from me…."

Examine God's indictment on the exceedingly religious but horribly unspiritual nation of Israel through the prophet Isaiah:

To what purpose is the multitude of your sacrifices unto me? saith the LORD: I am full of the burnt offerings of rams, and the fat of fed beasts; and I delight not in the blood of bullocks, or of lambs, or of he goats. When ye come to appear before me, who hath required this at your hand, to tread my courts? Bring no more vain oblations; incense is an abomination unto me; the new moons and sabbaths, the calling of assemblies, I cannot away with; it is iniquity, even the solemn meeting. Your new moons and your appointed feasts my soul hateth: they are a trouble unto me; I am weary to bear them. And when ye spread forth your hands, I will hide mine eyes from you: yea, when ye make many prayers, I will not hear: your hands are full of blood. Wash you, make you clean; put away the evil of your doings from before mine eyes; cease to do evil; Learn to do well; seek judgment, relieve the oppressed, judge the fatherless, plead for the widow.

Come now, and let us reason together, saith the LORD: though your sins be as scarlet, they shall be as white as snow; though they be red like crimson, they shall be as wool. If ye be willing and obedient, ye shall eat the good of the land: But if ye refuse and rebel, ye shall be devoured with the sword: for the mouth of the LORD hath spoken it.—ISAIAH 1:11–20

And finally, consider in Revelation, the Lord's words to the wonderfully busy church of Ephesus:

Unto the angel of the church of Ephesus write; These things saith he that holdeth the seven stars in his right hand, who walketh in the midst of the seven golden candlesticks; I know thy works, and thy labour, and thy patience, and how thou canst not bear them which are evil: and thou hast tried them which say they are apostles, and are not, and hast found them liars: And hast borne, and hast patience, and for my name's sake hast laboured, and hast not fainted. Nevertheless I have somewhat against thee, because thou hast left thy first love.—REVELATION 2:1–4

In each of these cases, people were serving, worshipping, and sacrificing unto the Lord. They were carrying out spiritual duties, but in every case, their motives were amiss. And God was obviously displeased.

What drives you? What causes you to wake up every day and live the Christian life or serve in Christian ministry? Are your motives pleasing to Christ, and are you driven by what drives Him?

Yes, motives matter. They matter deeply. Why? Because motives are the moorings of our lives with God, our hearts for Him, and our service unto Him. Wrong motives produce an empty life and a ministry that is not sustainable. Pure motives sustain our passion for God and thus sustain our work for Him—even during the dry, discouraging, or seemingly fruitless seasons of ministry.

No matter what area of responsibility we pursue, but especially in ministry, there are baser and greater motives that can prompt us to fulfill our God-given purposes. Simply put, living the Christian life or serving in ministry with less than pure and biblical motives produces fruitless, empty, and ultimately shipwrecked lives.

Over my life, personally and in ministry, I have often come face to face with impure motivations. At times God's Spirit has exposed them from within. Sometimes I have seen them in others. And occasionally, I have even heard them taught or preached.

Impure or lesser motivations include the following:

Guilt—Shame and guilt can be powerful motivators, but they won't sustain us for the long haul, and they won't fill us with the joy God desires us to have as we serve Him. Leading others to do right or serve God out of guilt is a losing proposition. This is the lowest form of motivation or spiritual leadership.

Opportunity—God opens doors of opportunity for all of us, but the availability of opportunity can never be our chief motivation. Often, the same doors that once were wide open eventually seem to close. When that happens, the same opportunity that was a motivator, can become a source of discouragement. Opportunity makes a weak motivation.

Money—Financial gain and money flow are unstable and unpredictable. If money is one of your chief motivators in ministry, you will face some serious ups and downs. Ministry can't be measured in dollars and cents, and it isn't to be undertaken "for filthy lucre" (1 Peter 5:2). Those who labor or live primarily for monetary reward are always ultimately and sorely disappointed.

Duty—Although we should give attention to our duties and be fully committed to God-given responsibilities, duty alone is a shallow motive. By itself, duty is a heartless, cold, and demanding taskmaster. A duty-bound spirit always struggles to radiate the joy and grace of the Christian life, the love of Jesus, and the presence of God.

Affirmation—We are commanded not to serve with "eyeservice, as menpleasers" (Colossians 3:22). In other words, we are not to be motivated by the need for appreciation, recognition, or praise of men. Affirmation is an odd and unpredictable blessing. Sometimes when you expect others to notice and comment on your work, their silence is discouraging. Other times, when you least expect it, you find reward or recognition for something you didn't even do.

It isn't wrong to receive affirmation, to be committed to your duty, to gain financial blessing, to accept an opportunity, or even to desire a clear conscience—but these are insufficient motivators. If these drive you in Christian living or ministry, you are setting yourself up for eventual failure.

These motivators hinge on human resources (either our own or someone else's) and fail to draw on the limitless passion that God desires to give His servants. As core reasons for ministry, they will not sustain us. And they will not fare well at the judgment seat of Christ.

So what are biblical motivations that can sustain us for a lifetime?

In the coming pages, I want to briefly share with you ten compelling reasons to faithfully serve the Lord. These are biblical, Christ-centered, and holy motivations. They flow from Scripture and from God's heart.

These are the ten motivators that truly keep me serving the Lord. They are also areas in which I am still growing and pursuing God and His will for my life. Over the past twenty-six years as pastor of Lancaster Baptist Church, I have at times been convicted that my service for the Lord has veered from its center target. More than a few times, I have experienced the conviction of God's Spirit when a motivation has slipped to a lower position. Each time the Holy Spirit realigns my focus and readjusts my motives, I'm strengthened, challenged, and inspired to pursue the excellence that Christ deserves.

Perhaps as you read, you will find many of these motivations already residing in your own heart, placed there by the Holy Spirit. Perhaps there will be a few motivators in these pages that will encourage you to readjust your focus.

Christ is worthy of our all—our purest love from our deepest devotion. He is worthy of our most passionate acts of service from our most sacred of motives.

I invite you to ponder with me the question, "Why do I do what I do?" Let's discover together ten sacred motivations for living for Christ and serving Him.

Not with eyeservice, as menpleasers; but as the servants of Christ, doing the will of God from the heart.

—Ephesians 6:6

THE GLORY OF GOD

Whether therefore ye eat, or drink, or whatsoever ye do,

do all to the glory of God.—1 CORINTHIANS 10:31

Sometimes we overcomplicate the Christian life. We develop formulas, lists, and philosophies, all of which may be good and helpful; but there is an overriding purpose to our lives, and it's quite simple—do all to the glory of God.

The word *glorify* means "to reveal or make clear." In simple terms, you and I were created for the express purpose of showing or revealing God more clearly to others. By our lives and very existence He should be seen more clearly—even magnified—in others' eyes. There is no higher motivation or purpose in all of life.

What a different and contrasting purpose than what we see in modern day pop culture. The message of the world is simply, "Glorify self!" The secular world idolizes mankind, magnifies the pleasure of man, and promotes the worship of self.

Romans 1 describes the godless, early Gentile world—a culture strikingly like our own.

> Because that, when they knew God, they glorified him not as God, neither were thankful; but became vain in their imaginations, and their foolish heart was darkened. Professing themselves to be wise, they became fools, And changed the glory of the uncorruptible God into an image made like to corruptible man, and to birds, and fourfooted beasts, and creeping things.—ROMANS 1:21–23

Today's systems around the world—from the educators to the Hollywood producers to the fashion designers to the musicians—are not concerned with glorifying God at all. In fact, as a whole, they "willingly are ignorant" of God (2 Peter 3:5).

Even in Christian ministry, there is much popular teaching about promoting self, building a brand, and developing a personal platform.

But for those of us who know God, and who have received Christ, our hearts' desire and purest passion should be to glorify Him—to make the Lord Jesus Christ more clearly known before men.

WHAT GLORIFIES GOD?

Every act of life—even eating and drinking—can be done "to the glory of God" (1 Corinthians 10:31). But God's Word shares particular activities or actions that are undeniably glorifying to God. When these are present in our lives, it is only because God is at work—for they are not natural. When these are present, they say loudly and clearly—God is at work!

Spiritual fruit glorifies God. John 15:8 says, "Herein is my Father glorified, that ye bear much fruit; so shall ye be my disciples." The fruit of our lives will be a witness for or against God's glory. John 15:4–5 teaches that as we abide in Christ, we can bear His fruit: "Abide in me, and I in you. As the branch cannot bear fruit of itself, except it abide in the vine; no more can ye, except ye abide in me. I am the vine, ye are the branches: He that abideth in me, and I in him, the same bringeth forth much fruit: for without me ye can do nothing."

That final phrase is a reminder to us that all the glory for spiritual fruit belongs to God. Just as it would be foolish for a branch in a vineyard to boast of its fruit (which could not have been produced without the vine nourishing the branch), so it is foolish for us to boast in our fruit-bearing accomplishments that are possible solely through Christ.

Spiritual fruit comes in two varieties—the fruit of the Holy Spirit flowing from our personalities and disposition into our relationships; and the fruit of leading others to the Lord through our personal witness.

Galatians 5:22–23 describes the fruit of the Holy Spirit: "But the fruit of the Spirit is love, joy, peace, longsuffering, gentleness, goodness, faith, Meekness, temperance: against such there is no law."

A Christian who evidences this fruit is a living testimony to God's power to transform the very nature of our lives—especially when the fruit of the Spirit is contrasted with the works of the flesh: "...Adultery, fornication, uncleanness, lasciviousness, Idolatry, witchcraft, hatred, variance, emulations, wrath, strife, seditions, heresies, Envyings, murders, drunkenness, revellings, and such like..." (Galatians 5:19–21).

Obviously, as seen in this passage, our natural fruit is anything but glorifying to God. We are broken, fallen creatures with sinful flesh that wants only to please and glorify itself. But God's Spirit within us generates a radically different kind of fruit. When His fruit abounds in our lives, it is obviously to God's glory!

Likewise, when we share the Gospel of Christ with a lost soul, we are engaging in the very act of "glorifying God." When that person prays to receive Christ as his personal Saviour, new fruit abounds to God's glory.

We see the Spirit's work in both our desire to share the Gospel and in the resulting fruit (Psalm 126:5–6). The Holy Spirit produces the loving compassion within us that compels us to share His Gospel with the lost. The resulting fruit brings glory to God.

Good works glorify God. In Matthew 5:16 Jesus instructed, "Let your light so shine before men, that they may see your good works, and glorify your Father which is in heaven."

Jesus is the Light that shines in darkness: "And the light shineth in darkness; and the darkness comprehended it not" (John 1:5). Christ's presence in us should illuminate the world for God. His light in us should enable others to see Him more clearly.

Sometimes it is simply our good response to a trial or our good works in the face of hardship that brings Him glory.

Consistent praise glorifies God. Psalm 22:23 says, "Ye that fear the LORD, praise him; all ye the seed of Jacob, glorify him; and fear him, all ye the seed of Israel." As we purposefully and specifically direct praise to God, we glorify Him.

God's glory as our highest motivation causes us to view His blessings through the lens of undeserving gratitude. Our response is then praise and thanksgiving to the Lord.

Generous giving glorifies God. First Chronicles 16:29 encourages, "Give unto the LORD the glory due unto his name: bring an offering, and come before him: worship the LORD in the beauty of holiness." Giving and worshipping are inseparably linked. We give to God to further His glory by ascribing worth to Him.

Presently our church is engaged in a 3.3-million-dollar building program which will expand our worship center and add new classrooms and an enlarged lobby. Against human reason, the Lord led us to begin this project in the middle of a long national recession. Frankly, it doesn't make sense. Yet in much prayer and consideration, we ventured out by faith. There is really only one reason we chose to do so—to glorify God.

As the theme for our giving program toward this effort, we chose "Elevate and Magnify," because we truly believe our sacrificial giving, the resulting provision of God, and the completion of the project will be only to the glory and magnification of God. There's no other explanation for what would motivate or enable a common group of people to come together for the building of such a structure. Giving to God, especially in lean times, gives great glory to Him!

If we desire to glorify God, we will want to purposefully participate in these actions that bring Him glory—leading others to Christ, submitting to the Holy Spirit's transforming work within us, doing good to others, praising the Lord, and giving to further God's work.

WHEN GOD'S GLORY MOTIVATES US

There is a difference in how we approach ministry when our highest motivation is God's glory. Below are some earmarks of ministry carried out to the glory of God.

We strive for excellence. Our God is excellent and worthy of our most excellent efforts. When His glory drives us, we dig deeper and strive to give Him our utmost in every area of life and service.

We live with integrity. When we care about God's glory, we strive for a deep level of authenticity in all of life, not just the visible aspects. God sees every part of our hearts and lives, and His glory calls us to absolute integrity and sincerity. His glory prohibits us from separating our lives into public and private—into ministry and non-ministry, holding each area to a different standard. God's glory calls us to integrity.

We care about the details. His glory changes how we handle the "insignificants." God's glory will motivate us to give attention to details we might dismiss were it only our own names at stake. What's "good enough" for me, may not be "good enough" for God's glory.

We are willing to be consumed for Christ. John the Baptist's highest ambition was to expend his life for Christ's glory. In John 3:30 he said, "He must increase, but I must decrease." John made Christ's magnification his life's mission, and he was satisfied by its completion. When God's glory becomes our motive—our passion—it is a joy to expend our lives for Christ alone.

ALL TO THE GLORY OF GOD

What is your highest motivation? What drives you right now? When God examines your heart's motives, does He find first and foremost a deep desire for His glory?

You were created for God's glory, and you're never more fully alive than when you are living to bring Him glory. And God is never more fully pleased than when your life is truly glorifying to Him!

⁂

SACRED MOTIVE #1
The Glory of God

Putting the Motive into Practice:

While God's glory is not the natural motivation of sinful man's life, it *was* God's original design—He created us to glorify Him. Below are some practical, purposeful steps you can take to structure your life in such a way that your heart's motive will turn from self-glory to God's glory.

List your current responsibilities or activities, and evaluate them by a standard of God's glory. If there are any that you could not do in good conscience to the glory of God, omit them from your life. Otherwise, note how you can promote God's glory through these activities.

Purposefully center your life on bearing fruit for Christ. Ask yourself if there are areas which you need to submit to the Holy Spirit so He can bear His fruit through you. Make time and create opportunities to personally witness to people who do not know the Lord, sharing with them the message of salvation.

Develop a habit of deflecting praise to God and others. When someone commends you for an achievement, give the glory to God and thank Him for the others whom He gave to provide help.

Strive for excellence in every area of your life and ministry. Step back periodically to view your responsibilities with a "first eye." How can you grow? How can you do a better job portraying the greatness of God?

Purposefully view the mundane as an opportunity for you to decrease so He might increase. Choose to do all things—even the common routines such as eating and drinking—to God's glory.

A LOST WORLD

Say not ye, There are yet four months, and then cometh
harvest? behold, I say unto you, Lift up your eyes, and
look on the fields; for they are white already to harvest.

—John 4:35

Years ago, our church began an effort to plant a church in Los
Angeles, California. Each weekend, we took groups of faithful
Christians downtown to knock on doors, share Christ, and invite
people to the Los Angeles Baptist Church.

One Saturday, I had the privilege of having Dr. Roland
Garlick, a longtime missionary to Mexico and a man greatly used
by God to preach the Gospel to the Spanish-speaking world, as my
doorknocking partner. I will never forget that day.

In his later years, Dr. Garlick was stricken with Parkinson's disease which caused him great discomfort and prolonged suffering. He often struggled to hold his head still as his neck muscles convulsed uncontrollably. Walking up stairs, standing to preach God's Word, and many other basic functions of ministry required tremendous effort. Yet, through all of his suffering, Dr. Garlick continued to faithfully proclaim God's Word and share the Gospel with the lost.

On this particular morning, after we had the privilege of knocking on many doors and leading several dear people to Jesus, Dr. Garlick paused to catch his breath. He was tired, but joyful, struggling, but overcoming. We stood on the sidewalk on Rampart Boulevard looking down the street toward the towering skyscrapers of Los Angeles.

Without warning, Dr. Garlick began to weep. As the tears flowed down his face, he softly said, "Brother Chappell, I don't know if you realize it, but Los Angeles is probably the single most unevangelized Spanish-speaking city in the world." He proceeded to name major Spanish-speaking cities around the world, citing their population and referencing the Gospel-preaching churches in each city. As he shared these statistics, he continued to weep for those who were yet waiting for the Gospel.

I clearly stood that day in the presence of a man who was deeply motivated by the lost souls of men. His heart mirrored Christ's heart.

If anyone had an excuse for self-pity, Dr. Garlick did. If anyone had a reason to rest, he did. If anyone could have justified "sitting out" on the Great Commission, he could have. But in spite of all the suffering and pain in his body, a deep motivation for the lost caused him to continue preaching the Gospel and weeping for the lost.

When we lose our perspective on the lost world around us, we lose the very purpose for ministry—the purpose for the local church. I don't merely believe in the *concept* of soulwinning. I believe it is the heart of Jesus for the local church.

In Matthew 28:18–20, Jesus "spake unto them, saying, All power is given unto me in heaven and in earth. Go ye therefore, and teach all nations, baptizing them in the name of the Father, and of the Son, and of the Holy Ghost: Teaching them to observe all things whatsoever I have commanded you: and, lo, I am with you alway, even unto the end of the world. Amen."

Christ's last command must be our first priority. But this should not just be a priority of mere obligation. It should be a genuine motive—a passion—for why we do what we do.

How can you restore your passion for a lost world?

SENSE THE URGENCY

Imagine you're a farmer surveying your fields on a hot, August day. Your harvest is mature and ready to be gathered, but storm clouds carrying large hailstones are rolling in. Although you may have machinery squeaking for repair and errands demanding attention, your highest priority today will be gathering your harvest before it is too late. At this point, the harvest is urgent.

This is the way Jesus saw people. In John 4:35, He said to His disciples, "Say not ye, There are yet four months, and then cometh harvest? behold, I say unto you, Lift up your eyes, and look on the fields; for they are white already to harvest."

The prophet Jeremiah also understood this urgency. God gives us a glimpse of his urgency as he mourned over those who delayed responding to God's message: "The harvest is past, the summer is ended, and we are not saved" (Jeremiah 8:20).

So it is for the soulwinner. The urgency of the harvest moves him to action.

Charles Spurgeon emphasized the urgency of the harvest with these words: "If sinners will be damned, at least let them leap into Hell over our bodies. And if they will perish, let them perish with our arms about their knees, imploring them to stay. If Hell must be filled, let not one go there unwarned and unprayed for."

I am blessed to have a godly grandmother. Not long ago, during her eighty-eighth year of life, she moved into a home not far from our family farm in Cortez, Colorado, but closer into town and more convenient for her needs. Shortly after she got settled in, a young family purchased and moved into a home on her street. Grandmother decided to welcome them by baking a pie, and as she delivered it, she sensed the Holy Spirit leading her to share the

Gospel. Within a short time, Grandmother led that young couple to Christ.

When she shared this story with me, she made this powerful statement, "Paul, I knew I needed to share the Lord with them because I know that I may not have another chance!" What a great motive! Who is it in your life who needs the Gospel? You may not have another chance.

REMEMBER ETERNITY

Sometimes we forget that every person we meet has an eternal soul that will live somewhere for ever. Scripture plainly states that those who do not trust Christ as Saviour will spend eternity in Hell (Revelation 20:15), and those who receive Christ's gift of salvation will spend eternity in Heaven (1 Peter 1:3–5).

Acts 4:12 states that salvation is exclusively available through Jesus Christ: "Neither is there salvation in any other: for there is none other name under heaven given among men, whereby we must be saved." Sometimes we become so concerned about appearing sensitive that we are unwilling to remember the severity of the situation.

If you were driving down the street and saw a house on fire, and the occupants were oblivious to the situation, what would you do? My guess is that you would worry very little about how your rescue efforts were perceived. You would probably be more concerned that your message is clear and that lives are saved!

And so it is in our personal soulwinning. When we truly become motivated by the eternal destinies of men, we will compassionately but courageously confront others with their need for Christ.

Recently at our church's missions conference, longtime missionary, Dr. Don Sisk, preached a message from Psalm 2:8 entitled "Who Wants the Heathen?" Sadly, Christians too often stand by as the heathen go to Hell. On your street, in your town, in cities around America, in countries around the world, there are billions of people without Christ and without hope. Remembering that their souls will live eternally motivates us to reach them with the Gospel. Remembering eternity motivates us to personal action—to speak to people about their souls, to give generously for mission efforts around the world. We can all do something. We must go. We must give. We must pray. People's eternity hangs in the balance.

PRAY FOR LABORERS

Jesus gave us a specific prayer request—one that pulses with the beat of His own heart. He requested that we pray for more laborers for the harvest of souls. In Matthew 9:37–38, He turned to His disciples and said, "The harvest truly is plenteous, but the labourers are few; Pray ye therefore the Lord of the harvest, that he will send forth labourers into his harvest."

Has this prayer request made it to your prayer list? Are you asking the Lord to raise up soulwinners with hearts of compassion for the lost?

One benefit of praying for this need is that it reminds us to personally labor in the harvest fields. It's difficult to pray very long for dedicated soulwinners without being compelled to win souls ourselves.

Another benefit is that praying on the behalf of a lost world stirs your own heart for their need. It reignites your passion and rekindles your motivation.

DEVELOP CHRIST'S COMPASSION

The heart of Christ, the supreme soulwinner, overflowed with compassion for the lost. We catch sight of this compassionate heart in Matthew 9:36: "But when he saw the multitudes, he was moved with compassion on them, because they fainted, and were scattered abroad, as sheep having no shepherd." Simply put, compassion moves us to passionate action. Genuine compassion will be tangibly expressed.

The compassion of the Lord moved Him to do something: "And Jesus, when he came out, saw much people, and was moved with compassion toward them, because they were as sheep not having a shepherd: and he began to teach them many things" (Mark 6:34).

Duty may compel you to attend a weekly visitation meeting and hand out tracts once a week—to fulfill your obligation. Compassion will motivate you to witness to others any time any where, simply because the love of Christ stirs your heart for the lost.

The Apostle Paul served out of this motivation. This motivation compelled him to witness for Christ during all seasons— not just at convenient moments. Even during a much-needed time of rest in Athens as he waited to be joined by his companions, he saw people through the eyes of compassion. Acts 17:16 records, "Now while Paul waited for them at Athens, his spirit was stirred in him, when he saw the city wholly given to idolatry."

Through the compassion of Christ, Paul saw the eternal needs of people, and his heart was stirred. Weary as he must have been, he couldn't help but share the truth with them.

Like first-century Athens, your community needs the Gospel. Christ's compassion through you will bring the sure result of fruitful soulwinning.

ANTICIPATE THE TROPHY

Compassionate soulwinning is an investment with guaranteed returns. Psalm 126:5–6 promises, "They that sow in tears shall reap in joy. He that goeth forth and weepeth, bearing precious seed, shall doubtless come again with rejoicing, bringing his sheaves with him."

At the end of life, our greatest joy will be wrapped up in those we led to Christ. Paul often expressed that those he had led to Christ and spiritually nurtured in discipleship were his "joy and crown"—his trophy.

> For what is our hope, or joy, or crown of rejoicing? Are not even ye in the presence of our Lord Jesus Christ at his coming?—1 THESSALONIANS 2:19

> Therefore, my brethren dearly beloved and longed for, my joy and crown, so stand fast in the Lord, my dearly beloved.—PHILIPPIANS 4:1

The ministry carries many administrative needs, and each of them is important. But it's easy to get buried in paperwork or lost in meetings and neglect the central purpose of the ministry—leading others to salvation.

Has the thought of anyone spending eternity in Hell motivated you recently? Have you grown cold toward the condition of lost men? How long has it been since you truly cared for another person's soul?

When you find yourself discouraged, weary, and lost in the fog of *why* you should remain faithful, you need a *reason* to continue serving Christ and living for Him. Someone's eternal destiny is the answer to your search for a reason to press on. Go—share the Gospel with a lost soul. Few things in all of life are as motivating and refreshing as seeing a man or woman, boy or girl, born into the family of God! There is nothing more valuable in life than the soul of a man!

SACRED MOTIVE #2
A Lost World

Putting the Motive into Practice:

What specific steps can you take to stir this motivation in your own heart?

Pray for Laborers. Start today to pray regularly that God would send forth laborers into the harvest. Pray that He would burden your heart and use you to lead others to Him.

Carry Gospel tracts and anticipate opportunities. Wake up tomorrow asking the Lord to give you opportunities to share Christ with others.

Express courage in the moment. When that opportunity to witness presents itself, step up in courage and confidence in Christ and share the truth. God will guide your words.

Maintain a prospect list. Keep a list of people you are praying for and actively sharing Christ with. Pray over that list every day. Reach out to people on that list every week.

Schedule specific times to get out of your comfort zone and share Christ. At least once a week or more, get out into your neighborhood, knock on some doors, introduce yourself, invite someone to your church, and seek to share the Gospel with people.

Expect fruit. In time, as you are faithful in these practices, God will give you fruit in the harvest!

SACRED MOTIVE

MY ACCEPTANCE IN CHRIST

To the praise of the glory of his grace, wherein he hath
made us accepted in the beloved.—EPHESIANS 1:6

You couldn't be any more loved by God than you are right
now. Does that statement strike a nerve of unrest with you? It's
absolutely true.

We all love affirmation. We all desire significance and
recognition. We all benefit from being encouraged by others. And
yet, this silent struggle for approval can often become an overriding motivation that keeps us on an unpredictable roller coaster
of insecurity and instability.

In truth, we crave the acceptance and approval of men, but
we *need* it from God. We long to know we matter to others, but

23

we forget how much we matter to Him. We desire approval and favor of our peers, but we lose sight of the approval and favor we already have in Christ. While we tend to seek these things from men, ultimately God is the only one in whom we can find our deepest desires completely fulfilled!

Satan is quick to take advantage of our need for acceptance and affirmation. He either enlarges our pride and consumes us with narcissism and self-promotion, or he reminds us of our failures and that we are insufficient and undeserving (which we are). In both extremes, Satan encourages us to indulge the flesh's craving for acceptance. It is easy to get caught in his trap of being motivated by the approval of others.

Through Ephesians 1, however, God graciously reminds us, "I love you and accept you through my Son, Jesus." Our worth is based on our birth. If you've been born again, you don't have anything to prove. You can't be any more loved than you are right now by the Lord Jesus Christ. Nothing you could do would cause Him to love you more or less. He loves you and accepts you fully and unconditionally. That's what grace is all about!

When God's grace—as opposed to our need for acceptance—becomes our motivator for service, everything changes. We serve *because* we are accepted rather than to *gain* acceptance—and it makes all the difference in the world.

SERVING BECAUSE I'M ALREADY ACCEPTED

Frankly, there have been times over the years when I was motivated, in part, by finding acceptance and approval from others. I know from experience that this is a futile motivation that is never wholly fulfilled. The most satisfying breakthroughs in my walk with God and my ministry for Him have come when He reminded me that I'm free to serve because I'm already accepted, not because I need to gain acceptance.

In truth, the tendency to serve for others' approval is a lifelong battle. And learning to rest in our acceptance in Christ is a lifelong growth process.

There were three major seasons and three vital areas early in my ministry when the Lord taught me to serve Him out of the joy of knowing I am accepted rather than for the desire to become accepted. These were difficult moments—times when God wrenched impure motives out of my hands and replaced them with purer aims.

The Affirmation of Mentors

First, one of the strongest mentors in my life left the ministry under a cloud. This was a man from whom I longed for acceptance and approval. I often called him to report what God was doing in my life and ministry—hoping he would be pleased. But when he left the ministry, I remember crying myself to sleep every night for six weeks.

For months, I wrestled with my motives. In this time of heartbreaking disappointment, I found I had lost my desire to press forward—I didn't want to preach, win souls, serve, or grow. Suddenly, the motivation that had driven me for years was stripped away. It was almost like none of it mattered anymore.

But in His grace, God showed me that it did all still matter. It simply mattered for higher reasons! The Lord taught me during that time that I needed to die to self. He convicted me that affirmation and ego needs are indicators of a self-driven person. He called me away from those impure motives and settled my spirit in His unchanging acceptance.

The Affirmation of Peers

When our family first moved to Lancaster, the church was running less than twenty. In those early days, other pastors would sometimes call to tell me they were praying for us and ask how it was going. I was thankful for these godly friends, and I longed to give them good reports.

As God began to bless the ministry, I remember the thrill of sharing each new phase of growth—"We had thirty in church this Sunday!" And a few months later, "We filled the middle section of pews!" My friends would rejoice with me in the growth God was giving, and I was thankful for their prayers and support.

After a number of years, however, a strange shift took place. As I reported new growth and attendance numbers—numbers nearing the attendance of the pastors who were my friends—the response became less enthusiastic. What had been an excited "Really? That's awesome, brother!" became a short "Glad to hear it." Then, as our attendance surpassed others, the calls became less frequent. Eventually, they halted altogether.

Over time, men who once invited me to preach and fellowship with them grew silent and disinterested. Those from whom I wanted acceptance and affirmation were no longer giving it. And frankly, this hurt. I had looked to these partners in ministry for encouragement and support, and for whatever reason, our friendships grew distant, and in some cases even hurtful.

Through all of this, the Lord again said, "I'm teaching you to find your acceptance in Me alone. You serve not to seek acceptance, but because you are already accepted—in Me!"

The Affirmation of Those I Served

For many years in ministry, God gave me a sort of "honeymoon" experience. As people came to Christ and lives were changed, the church came alive with a loving and dynamic spirit. I loved our church family, and they loved me. That's how it should be, but for me, this was often a motivator. Being accepted by the church family was a wonderfully encouraging and affirming experience. The security of this strong and loving relationship is a blessing, but it should not be a motivation.

This unhealthy motivation didn't reveal itself until the 1990s when a few people in our church let me know—in no uncertain terms—that they were unhappy with me. Their anger cut me to the core, and I grieved deeply from it. Yet, through the tears the Lord taught me, "It's not about who accepts you; it's about Who already accepted you."

These were important (and painful) lessons—and honestly the Lord is still teaching me in all of these areas.

As you serve the Lord in your own place, ask Him to reveal to you areas in which you're seeking for the affirmation and approval of others. In Christ, we have all the acceptance we need. But sometimes we miss the joy of basking in His acceptance because we are preoccupied with grasping for the acceptance of other people.

A HOSTAGE TO THE APPROVAL OF OTHERS

The impure motive of seeking the acceptance of others is often layered beneath seemingly godly ambitions. As we close this chapter, consider a few indicators that might reveal that you are a hostage to the approval of others.

Guilt or Comparison with Others

Is your schedule drawn out of guilt? Do you drive yourself forward because you fear that you are not keeping pace with others? Do you find yourself deeply discouraged because your ministry results look different than those of someone else?

> For we dare not make ourselves of the number, or compare ourselves with some that commend themselves: but they measuring themselves by themselves, and comparing themselves among themselves, are not wise.—2 CORINTHIANS 10:12

> And whatsoever ye do, do it heartily, as to the Lord, and not unto men;—COLOSSIANS 3:23

Overwhelming Frustration at Our Inability

God allows weakness in our lives to enlarge our capacity for His strength. Yet, when we are seeking the affirmation of others, we become frustrated and impatient with our own limitations. When we are self-driven, we miss ministering by God's grace, and that scenario always creates deep frustration.

Yes, the Christian whose heart burns for God's glory will always desire to do more for Christ. Remembering our position in Christ will encourage us to do it in *His* strength alone.

In his book *Lectures to My Students*, Charles Spurgeon wrote, "When your own emptiness is painfully forced upon your consciousness, chide yourself that you ever dreamed of being full except in the Lord."

> And he said unto me, My grace is sufficient for thee: for my strength is made perfect in weakness. Most gladly therefore will I rather glory in my infirmities, that the power of Christ may rest upon me. Therefore I take pleasure in infirmities, in reproaches, in necessities, in persecutions, in distresses for Christ's sake: for when I am weak, then am I strong.—2 CORINTHIANS 12:9–10

Discouragement in the Face of Criticism

Some of the greatest advice I've ever been given was from Dr. Lee Roberson when he told me, "Die to self! Die to criticism; die to praise." Criticism is painful, and it hurts me deeply. Often, the Lord convicts me that the pain of criticism is an indicator that I'm more concerned about what others think of me than I should be. In reality, the pain of criticism is often driven by the sharp barb of pride.

> I am crucified with Christ: nevertheless I live; yet not I, but Christ liveth in me: and the life which I now live in the flesh I live by the faith of the Son of God, who loved me, and gave himself for me.—GALATIANS 2:20

ENJOYING YOUR POSITION

The joy of being "accepted in the beloved" refers to far more than salvation alone. It means that you are "in Christ." This is a literal spiritual position that makes the sufficiency of His grace available to us every moment of every day. It means Christ truly is my all in all!

The Christian life is designed to be a life of unity and union with Christ. Because we are "in Christ," we share His death and resurrection. In Christ, the enthronement of self ends. In Him we have the ability to reckon ourselves dead to sin, self, and our carnal tendencies, and to live in the power of the Resurrection (Romans 6:11).

As Paul recognized the truth that his old man was crucified with Christ, he expressed his passion to live for God—"nevertheless I live!" God does not expect the Christian life to be lived by the ability and power of the flesh, but by the power of the living Spirit of God. The indwelling Spirit gives us a passion to live for God moment by moment.

The Holy Spirit also gives us a passionate hunger to experience the daily presence of God. Galatians 2:20 reminds us that we don't live the Christian life in our own strength, but "Christ liveth in me."

How do we daily live out the life of Christ? By faith. By trusting and resting in the knowledge that we are fully accepted by Him and fully yielded to Him as He lives His life through us: "...the life which I now live in the flesh I live by the faith of the Son of God, who loved me, and gave himself for me" (Galatians 2:20). Christ's incredible sacrifice for us motivates us to live for Him by faith.

Are you motivated in life and ministry by a need for the acceptance or affirmation you receive from others? Are you driven by a desire for recognition? This motivation will lead you to disappointment.

Wake up tomorrow with a fresh motivation—remember anew that you are fully accepted and loved by Jesus Christ, and let all of His life begin flowing from you unhindered by personal ego or pride.

SACRED MOTIVE #3

My Acceptance in Christ

Putting the Motive into Practice

Internalizing this motivation is more about accepting a mindset than it is about acting on specifics. As you ask the Lord to help you become motivated by His unconditional acceptance, take a moment to consider God's Word to you:

My Position in Christ—Romans 8

- No condemnation in Christ Jesus—8:1
- We are freed from the law of sin and death—8:2
- We have the Spirit dwelling in us—8:9–10

- Our mortal bodies will be quickened—8:11
- We are joint heirs with Christ—8:17
- We know all things work together for good—8:28
- We know His purpose is for us to be conformed to Christ—8:29
- God is for us who are in Christ—8:31
- We are freely given all things through Christ—8:32
- We are justified—3:24–25; 8:33
- We have an intercessor—8:34
- We cannot be separated from His love—8:35–39

My Position in Christ—Ephesians 1 and 2

- We are blessed with all spiritual blessings—1:3
- We are positioned in the heavenly places—1:3
- We are chosen to be without blame before Him—1:4
- We are adopted as children—1:5
- We are accepted—1:6
- We are redeemed through His blood—1:7
- We are forgiven of our sins—1:7
- We are shown His will as He purposed in Himself—1:9–10
- We have obtained an inheritance—1:11
- We are the praise of His glory—1:12
- We are sealed by His Spirit—1:13
- We are given security of our inheritance—1:14
- We are His workmanship—2:10
- We are made nigh by His blood and we have peace—2:13–14

THE WORD OF GOD

For whatsoever things were written aforetime were written for our learning, that we through patience and comfort of the scriptures might have hope.—ROMANS 15:4

In a given year in America, hundreds of thousands of new books enter the marketplace. Many of these books are self-help books—written and marketed with the promise of change, improvement, and a better life. Americans have an unquenchable thirst to better themselves, because they have a deep, nagging discontentment with who they are and where they are in life.

The sad news is that the multi-million-dollar self-help industry is successful, but its strategies are not. Its very success is founded upon the fact that new books, new diets, new strategies, and new promises are needed annually. Today's strategies don't work any better than yesterday's strategies—but they sell well.

Deep within every man and woman is the knowledge that we are broken—that we desperately need improvement and personal change. New year's resolutions, tactics of personal discipline, and strategies of positive thinking only take us so far. They remake the externals, for a season, but they are powerless in truly transforming us internally. For all of our medical and psychological research, for all of our magazines, books, talk shows, and treatment centers, for all of our seminars, strategies, and schemes for personal satisfaction, we are all the more empty and hopeless.

If you are looking to a new book, a new diet, or a new self-help philosophy to motivate you, this is a path of disappointment.

But there is one book—one source of truth that is eternally transforming and ultimately motivating. It is a living book—a life-changing book. It is a book that will discern your heart and transform your thinking every time you open it. It is a book that will make good on every one of its promises. It will never fail and never be found insufficient.

The Word of God is one of the greatest motivators in all of life!

THE BIBLE IS "MY BOOK"

Years ago, as a Bible college student pastoring on weekends, I was privileged to lead a man to the Lord. He had been searching for answers in all the wrong places and had finally come to the end of himself. Shortly after he trusted Jesus as his Saviour, he began to walk personally with the Lord and read God's Word. Over the months, the change he had long sought after was beginning to unfold in his heart. This was true and lasting change—transformation generated by the very words of God.

I was delighted to receive a letter from him several months after he began to follow the Lord. He recounted the great joy of being saved and the marvelous change God was creating in his life. But one sentence of the letter jumped off the page at me. He simply stated, "The Bible is my book…I read it often!"

No wonder this man was experiencing radical life change. No wonder he was becoming a different man. It wasn't because he had enlisted in a personal improvement seminar or bought the next "How to Be the Best You" book. As a new Christian he had made a critical decision. The Bible became his primary book. The Word of God became one of his greatest sources of motivation.

Is the Bible your book? Do you read it often? Or have you become bored and disconnected from its transforming truth?

GOD'S WORD CHANGES US

Every part of my life has been radically and undeniably changed by the Word of God. Looking back over four decades of Christian living, I can trace every major decision, every abundant blessing, and every critical turning point directly to the Word of God. Thousands of times, using His Word through reading, studying, hearing teaching, and hearing preaching (even as a child), God has dramatically altered my life and direction.

God's Word has the power to stir, to change, and to motivate like no human device can. God Himself speaks to us through its pages—breathing fresh truth, courage, strength, and hope into our souls. And every time we open God's Word, we avail ourselves of the very presence and power of God—it is a living, breathing book "which effectually worketh also in you that believe" (1 Thessalonians 2:13).

This promise simply means, that as I read God's Word with a believing and receptive heart, it works in me in ways I cannot see or feel. It effectually brings about personal transformation—renewing my mind, reconstructing my thoughts, rebuilding my character, and revising my behavior. God's Word always works to mold me into the image of Jesus Christ. Every time I open the Bible, I am lying down on God's surgical table and allowing Him to do a spiritual and eternal work in my heart. And the Word of God never returns void—it always accomplishes that which it was purposed to accomplish (Isaiah 55:11).

THE POWERFUL AND POSITIVE EFFECTS OF THE BIBLE

Throughout Scripture, God tells us many specific blessings that come to our lives through His Word.

God's Word was given by God and is profitable. "All scripture is given by inspiration of God, and is profitable for doctrine, for reproof, for correction, for instruction in righteousness" (2 Timothy 3:16).

God's Word is alive and discerns our hearts. "For the word of God is quick, and powerful, and sharper than any twoedged sword, piercing even to the dividing asunder of soul and spirit, and of the joints and marrow, and is a discerner of the thoughts and intents of the heart" (Hebrews 4:12).

God's Word effectually works in us. "For this cause also thank we God without ceasing, because, when ye received the word of God which ye heard of us, ye received it not as the word of men, but as it is in truth, the word of God, which effectually worketh also in you that believe" (1 Thessalonians 2:13).

God's Word gives us patience, comfort, and hope. "For whatsoever things were written aforetime were written for our learning, that we through patience and comfort of the scriptures might have hope" (Romans 15:4).

God's Word is perfect, sure, right, and pure. "The law of the LORD is perfect, converting the soul: the testimony of the LORD is sure, making wise the simple. The statutes of the LORD are right, rejoicing the heart: the commandment of the LORD is pure, enlightening the eyes" (Psalm 19:7–8).

God's Word purifies our lives. "Wherewithal shall a young man cleanse his way? by taking heed thereto according to thy word" (Psalm 119:9).

God's Word enlightens and directs our paths. "Thy word is a lamp unto my feet, and a light unto my path" (Psalm 119:105).

God's Word protects us from offense. "Great peace have they which love thy law: and nothing shall offend them" (Psalm 119:165).

God's Word gives true success and prosperity. "This book of the law shall not depart out of thy mouth; but thou shalt meditate therein day and night, that thou mayest observe to do according to all that is written therein: for then thou shalt make thy way prosperous, and then thou shalt have good success" (Joshua 1:8).

God's Word gives understanding. "The fear of the LORD is the beginning of wisdom: and the knowledge of the holy is understanding" (Proverbs 9:10). "The entrance of thy words giveth light; it giveth understanding unto the simple" (Psalm 119:130).

God's Word is eternally valuable. "The words of the LORD are pure words: as silver tried in a furnace of earth, purified seven times" (Psalm 12:6).

When you are weary, God's Word will encourage you. When you seek answers, God's Word will guide you. When you need strength, God's Word will revive you. When you face a trial, God's Word will sustain you. When you enter into despair, God's Word will give you hope. When you need wisdom, God's Word will enlighten you. When you need to know God's heart, God's Word will lead you. When you wander away from Jesus, God's Word will find you and show you the path back home.

WHERE DO YOU TURN?

Where do you turn for renewal? Where do you look for answers? Where do you seek change and personal growth? Too many Christians have become bored and disconnected from their most vital source of nourishment and motivation. Too often we turn first to our own devices, and God's Word becomes our last thought.

Are you allowing God's priceless Word to be replaced or undermined by other influences in your life—internet philosophy, apathy, distraction, neglect? When you have a serious question about life, do you think "Google" before you think "Bible?" Seeking and understanding God's truth should be our first thought in all of life's questions.

Proverbs 2:1–6 promises, "My son, if thou wilt receive my words, and hide my commandments with thee; So that thou incline thine ear unto wisdom, and apply thine heart to understanding; Yea, if thou criest after knowledge, and liftest up thy voice for understanding; If thou seekest her as silver, and searchest for her as for hid treasures; Then shalt thou understand the fear of the LORD, and find the knowledge of God. For the LORD giveth wisdom: out of his mouth cometh knowledge and understanding."

Anchor your life to God's Word. Immerse your heart into His truth. Schedule time daily to read it, memorize it, and meditate upon it. Allow His words to become the foundation of your life. In so doing, you will find a deep spiritual motivation and transformation that nothing else can provide. Truly this is the path to "good success!"

> This book of the law shall not depart out of thy mouth; but thou shalt meditate therein day and night, that thou mayest observe to do according to all that is written therein: for then thou shalt make thy way prosperous, and then thou shalt have good success.—Joshua 1:8

SACRED MOTIVE #4
The Word of God

Putting the Motive into Practice:

With the incredible, incomparable, incomprehensible treasure of God's Word available at our very fingertips, how specifically do we allow it to motivate our lives and propel our service for God?

Regularly spend personal time with God through His Word. As we serve others, there is often the temptation to forgo our own personal time with the Lord. Resist this tendency, and instead purposefully schedule time to daily steep your mind in God's Word. Read it, study it, memorize it, apply it, and, above all, seek God through it. God reveals Himself to us through His Word, and as we seek His face through the pages of Scripture, He draws nigh to us.

Meditate on what God promises is available through His Word. Remembering the treasures contained in Scripture will motivate you to personally seek these blessings for yourself. Perhaps you could memorize the verses listed in this chapter on the powerful and positive effects of the Bible. Read Psalm 19 and discover specifically how God uses His Word in our lives. Study Psalm 119 and note the many ways which God's Word impacts our lives, and what a treasure it is to those who love it.

Periodically take a personal inventory of specific ways that God has recently changed your life through His Word. The inspired words of God have the power to transform our lives—our thoughts, habits, desires, choices, patterns of living. But this only happens if we give God's Word entrance into our lives. As you periodically pause to list positive changes God has brought into your life over the past weeks or months, two blessings are possible: First, you will rejoice at what God has done in your life and will grow in your love for God's Word. Or you will see that—while you may have been around Scripture—you have not been recently changed by its truths. This can prompt you to search your heart and renew your hunger for truth-effected change in your life.

Purposefully center your ministry around God's Word. Truly, we have nothing to give others outside of the truth of God. And one of the most energizing experiences in ministry is watching the Word of God at work in another person's life. In whatever place and capacity and people you serve—in your home, in providing counseling, in preaching, in teaching, in personal ministry—let God's Word be the center. Efforts to help others that are absent of God's truth are shallow and short-lived. But ministry empowered by God's Spirit and filled with His Word brings life, hope, and lasting change.

THE LOVE OF CHRIST

For the love of Christ constraineth us; because we thus judge, that if one died for all, then were all dead: And that he died for all, that they which live should not henceforth live unto themselves, but unto him which died for them, and rose again.—2 CORINTHIANS 5:14–15

Alexander Solzhenitsyn was a Russian writer who resisted the rise of communism in the Soviet Union thoughout the last half of the twentieth century. He was unjustly imprisoned, and then, shortly before his release, sentenced for life to the Gulag, the Soviet Union's forced labor camp system. He wrote extensively of his suffering and received the Nobel Prize in literature in 1970.

During Solzhenitsyn's imprisonment, he came to personal faith in Jesus Christ. His encounter with the love of Christ, in the midst of such dark and hopeless circumstances, continually infused his heart with hope and strength.

At one point he became so weak and discouraged that he wished to die. After watching many men die from the brutal beatings of the prison guards, Alexander made a difficult decision. He decided to give up—to stop working. This would cause the guards to beat him to death. In comparison to his suffering, death was a welcomed freedom.

Sensing his despair, another Christian friend in the same prison discreetly drew a cross in the dirt where he knew Alexander would see it. That cross changed everything. For Alexander, the image crudely carved into the dirt provided a fresh reminder of the Saviour who loved him.

In the most desperate of circumstances, Alexander Solzhenitsyn found new strength and fresh hope. Remembering the love of Jesus changed everything.

Love is one of the purest and greatest motivators in all of life. When you love someone, you are highly motivated to express that love. When you know someone loves you, you are highly motivated to honor that love.

LOSS OF MOTIVATION IS OFTEN A LOSS OF LOVE

If you find yourself lacking motivation, or struggling with wrong motivations, there's a very good chance you've lost perspective of the love of Christ—both His love for you and your love for Him.

The church at Ephesus experienced this problem. In their busyness and labor for the Lord, they became motivated and driven by lesser loves—things that took the place of their highest love for Christ. They lost sight of their first love:

> Unto the angel of the church of Ephesus write; These things saith he that holdeth the seven stars in his right hand, who walketh in the midst of the seven golden candlesticks; I know thy works, and thy labour, and thy patience, and how thou canst not bear them which are evil: and thou hast tried them which say they are apostles, and are not, and hast found them liars: And hast borne, and hast patience, and for my name's sake hast laboured, and hast not fainted. Nevertheless I have somewhat against thee, because thou hast left thy first love. Remember therefore from whence thou art fallen, and repent, and do the first works; or else I will come unto thee quickly, and will remove thy candlestick out of his place, except thou repent.—REVELATION 2:1–5

This was a church of faithful Christians who were diligent in service. Yet, even in the midst of their fervency, Jesus declared that He found them lacking in their first love. They lost sight of what it was all about—Jesus' love for us, and our love for Him. This love is the centerpiece of the Christian life. This is the foundation of our relationship with Jesus—He loves us, and He desires our love in return.

Apart from the love of Christ, lesser motivations leave our Christian walk and service both empty and pointless. We find ourselves aimlessly repeating religious routines and offering sentimental sacrifices that amount to nothing but sounding brass and tinkling cymbals (1 Corinthians 13:1). A loveless Christian life is no life at all.

A LIFETIME OF MOTIVATION

The author of the book of Hebrews was writing to develop mature faith in Hebrew Christians. He was calling new believers away from their religiosity and systematic scheduled worship and into an intimate, ongoing relationship with Jesus. He was radically dismantling everything they knew—or thought they knew about God; and he was replacing all of their systematic perspective with a relational perspective of a Saviour that is more wonderful and personal than they ever imagined.

In chapter twelve, he presents the readers with an eternally motivating, heavenly perspective on the love of Christ:

> Wherefore seeing we also are compassed about with so great a cloud of witnesses, let us lay aside every weight, and the sin which doth so easily beset us, and let us run with patience the race that is set before us, Looking unto Jesus the author and finisher of our faith; who for the joy that was set before him endured the cross, despising the shame, and is set down at the right hand of the throne of God. For consider him that endured such contradiction of sinners against himself, lest ye be wearied and faint in your minds.—HEBREWS 12:1–3

Think about these phrases, "looking unto Jesus…" and "consider him…." When you are tempted and weighed down—when your motivation for running the race grows weak, look to Jesus. Remember the cross. Consider His love, His sacrifice, His grace. Consider what He endured for you. Remember the passionate love He expressed toward you from that excruciating place of death and sin.

Trace His bloody steps from the agonizing garden prayer to the beating and flogging by Roman guards to the mock trial to the weighty walk under a heavy cross and, ultimately, to the place of crucifixion. Remember that the hands that fashioned the universe were willingly opened for the Roman nails. Remember the heart that wept for Jerusalem was lifted up and driven through with a soldier's spear. Consider the brow that bore the thorns and the back that was opened by the cat-of-nine-tails. Remember the crowds that scorned and the blood that flowed. And perhaps, most of all, remember the perfect, eternal Son of God crying out, "My God, my God, why hast thou forsaken me!" as He who knew no sin literally became sin for us (2 Corinthians 5:21).

What is man that God would demonstrate such love? And how could any man partaking of that love return anything less than the highest love—with all our heart, mind, soul, and body?

Truly, "...the love of Christ constraineth us..." (2 Corinthians 5:14). One glimpse of the cross is enough for a lifetime of motivation. When we struggle for a reason to press on, a reason to do right, a reason to be faithful—we only need to look at the cross. When we consider Him, everything comes into focus. The love of Christ calls us to a deep devotion that defies all desperation.

How often we turn inward and become self-centered—introspective to a fault. How often our eyes fall from the cross to our circumstances. Our minds forget, our hearts are distracted, and our motivations diminish. Our spiritual attention spans can be rather short. Perhaps this is the reason Jesus commanded us in 1 Corinthians 11 to regularly take time through the Lord's Table to remember Him.

In the shadow of the cross, the burdens of life and ministry seem to pale. That which seemed utterly overwhelming and discouraging suddenly seems but a small taste of what it means to truly "take up your cross." The hope offered to us through the redemptive relationship we have with Christ infuses the most discouraged heart with new strength and desire.

VIEWING EVERY TRIAL THROUGH THE LOVE OF CHRIST

Paul never got over the fact that the Son of God had personally died for his sin. He was continually motivated and constrained by that love. It drove him to endure much personal persecution and suffering (2 Corinthians 11:23–28). It kept him focused on his call and dependent upon Christ's strength. He saw every trial through the lens of Christ's love and therefore was able to remain faithful, knowing that even his most difficult trial was helping to mature young Christians as they saw Christ's life and love in him. Here's how he stated it:

> We are troubled on every side, yet not distressed; we are perplexed, but not in despair; Persecuted, but not forsaken; cast down, but not destroyed; Always bearing about in the body the dying of the Lord Jesus, that the life also of Jesus might be made manifest in our body. For we which live are alway delivered unto death for Jesus' sake, that the life also of Jesus might be made manifest in

our mortal flesh. So then death worketh in us, but life in you.—2 CORINTHIANS 4:8–12

Imagine how every day of your life would be different if you had the perspective of the Apostle Paul—if every circumstance was received through the lens of the love of Christ. Consider how your heart would be strengthened if even in the most difficult of circumstances you knew God was using you to help others understand and experience His love.

FICKLE MOTIVATIONS

We all have good days and bad days. We all experience days when things seem to go well for us, and others when nothing seems to go right. Even in Christian ministry, there are regular ups and downs— some days people seem to be growing in God's grace and maturing in His love, and others days people seem to be carnal and contentious. If our heart motives are in any way connected to favorable circumstances or friendly people, we are in for certain disappointment.

Sacred motivations are not fickle. They are transcendent! They are not dependent upon the behavior of others or the predictability of our days. Sacred motivations are resting upon higher values and fixed promises. And there is no higher, more sacred, or more fixed value than the unconditional, unchanging, abundant love of Jesus Christ.

The faithfulness of circumstances or people is unpredictable, but the faithfulness of Jesus is unchanging.

If you are facing a moment when you wonder how to take another step—look to the cross. When you lack the strength and motivation to go forward for God—consider Him. When you feel alone, unloved, and unable—remember that He loves you, and you love Him—and that's really all you need!

SACRED MOTIVE #5

The Love of Christ

Putting the Motive into Practice:

First John 4:19 says, "We love him, because he first loved us." Christ's sacrificial love for us stirs our hearts to love Him in return. Below are suggested ways to kindle your love for Christ by remembering His love for you.

Meditate on the love of Christ for you. Read through the four gospels—Matthew, Mark, Luke, and John—paying special attention to the love God expressed through sending Christ to this world. Particularly, as you read these four accounts of Jesus' crucifixion, you will be reminded of the height, depth, length, and breadth of His love.

Verbally tell the Lord you love Him. Even in human relationships, reaffirming love with the simple words "I love you" strengthens that love. Telling the Lord that you love Him is not only a joy to Him, it can be a motivator to you.

Express love through the routine or unpleasant. True love is not just a sentiment—it is a verb. And the Christian who is consumed with love for Christ will see even routine, mundane tasks as opportunities to demonstrate love for Him.

Love the unlovely in Christ's name. Christ did not love us because we were lovely, but because He is love. Once we have trusted Him as our Saviour and are filled with His love, we have the ability to offer that love to others. Those who are constrained and motivated by the love of Christ do not limit their love to those who seem worthy or grateful; they seek out the unlovely and minister to them in Jesus' name.

THE LOCAL CHURCH

Take heed therefore unto yourselves, and to all the flock,
over the which the Holy Ghost hath made you overseers,
to feed the church of God, which he hath purchased with
his own blood.—Acts 20:28

I read the story of a young girl's first Sunday in "big church" with
her mother. She was excited about this special moment and was
quiet and still right up to the closing prayer. But as the pastor
prayed, "Lord, we thank Thee for your presence," she could contain
herself no longer. Her eyes flew open, and she pulled her mother's
sleeve. "Mommy, are we gonna get presents?!"

Yes, indeed. Every good gift and every perfect gift comes from
our Heavenly Father (James 1:17). He is the one who gives us all

things richly to enjoy (1 Timothy 6:17). He is a loving and a giving God, and one of the greatest gifts He has ever given to us is the ministry of the local church.

I'm partial to this chapter because I truly love the local church. I love everything about it. One of the most frustrating experiences of my life and ministry has been to watch our church outgrow my ability to physically be at every event and every function—I love it all!

When I have a visitor who comes to church, I want to show him everything on campus—right down to the closets. I want to sit him down and tell him the miracles that God has unfolded in our church and in my life through our church. I want him to trust Jesus and immerse his life into the church as I have—and to reap the multiple benefits of total commitment to the institution for which Jesus died.

I like church buildings, church landscaping, church architecture, church bulletins, church curriculum, church instruments, church busses, church potlucks, church mission conferences, church families—I just like church!

I believe in the local New Testament church, and I believe it is God's entity through which He changes lives today. The local church is His idea and His ordained method of reaching the lost with the Gospel and seeing them become rooted and grounded disciples of Jesus.

The local church embodies God's process of communicating truth to human hearts—His way of helping every individual know how to live, how to have joy, and how to know Christ. Through the local church, the Word of God is connected to needy hearts. Men and women become children of God. Husbands and wives discover how to love and care for each other as Christ does the church. Dads and moms discover how to nurture and train up their children in the ways of Scripture. Young men and young ladies grow up in the knowledge of Christ, established upon the strong foundation of His truth. Without the church, these things just don't happen anywhere else in today's culture.

And when I think of things that stir me—that motivate me at my core—I think of the local church. What happens at church is eternal. It is of highest value. The worship, the preaching, the fellowship, the ministry that unfolds in local churches, ignite my heart to serve and live for my Saviour.

THE CHURCH MOTIVATED JESUS

Christ died to purchase the church—she is His bride. Ephesians 5:25–27 says, "Husbands, love your wives, even as Christ also loved the church, and gave himself for it; That he might sanctify and cleanse it with the washing of water by the word, That he might present it to himself a glorious church, not having spot, or wrinkle, or any such thing; but that it should be holy and without blemish."

Think of the passion with which a groom loves his bride. Think of the attraction and commitment. This picture is but a glimpse of the unspeakable love Jesus has for the church. The hope of redeeming the souls of men and establishing His church literally drove Him to the cross. He loved the church so much that He gave His life for it (Acts 20:28).

We are His bride. He died for us. He made us members one of another. He brought us together in local bodies for the purpose of worshipping Him, serving Him, reaching the world, and edifying one another. What a privilege! What a high calling it is to be a part of the body of Christ and called to serve Him and one another.

There's a lot being written today about church ministry. Some are declaring its demise. They teach that the local church is a failed proposition—a flawed entity that needs to be abandoned for newer and more creative methods of evangelism and life change. Literally, every twenty years or so Christendom becomes bored with its present strategies and launches into yet another effort to reinvent and re-engineer Jesus' bride. This is nothing less than an ill-conceived assault on God's original design.

The local church, as it functioned in the New Testament, is still alive and well. It doesn't need to be reinvented or re-engineered. It simply needs to be revived. God's pattern of local church ministry is as effective today as it was in the first century. It works, but not because of our strategies, statistics, and studies. It works, but not because of our intellect or intelligence. It works, but not because of our masterful marketing strategies.

It works because God has ordained it by His power and grace. He has chosen to build His church. He has declared that the gates of Hell will not prevail against it. It is perpetuated and preserved, not by our strategy, but by His sovereignty. The biblical, local church is no more in danger of obsolescence than the promises of God are.

It is true that we are living in a "lukewarm" age. It is true, that compromise and complacency are everywhere. It is true, that many so-called churches are failing to uphold the truth and develop devoted followers of Christ. But there is still a host of Bible-believing Christians all over the world who are growing in local churches—loving Jesus, loving one another, and loving lost souls.

The church is safe, secure, and strong. Why do I know this?

1. **Because Jesus owns the church**
   Take heed therefore unto yourselves, and to all the flock, over the which the Holy Ghost hath made you overseers, to feed the church of God, which he hath purchased with his own blood.—Acts 20:28

2. **Because Jesus is the cornerstone**
   And are built upon the foundation of the apostles and prophets, Jesus Christ himself being the chief corner stone.—Ephesians 2:20

3. **Because Jesus will protect the church**

> And I say also unto thee, That thou art Peter, and upon this rock I will build my church; and the gates of hell shall not prevail against it.—Matthew 16:18

Just as the church motivated Jesus—it should motivate us as well. What could be more stirring to the heart than to partner with Jesus Christ in His eternal work unfolding on Earth?

THE PRIORITY OF THE LOCAL CHURCH

If the church was worthy of the shed blood of Jesus Christ, then the church is worthy of my commitment and time. What could be a higher priority in your week than what is happening through the power of the Gospel in your local church? What could be a higher priority than the eternal salvation of the lost?

I recently came across this simple but humorous comparison of church and sporting events. It pointedly exposes how we are often motivated by lesser things, and how easily we allow something as valuable as the bride of Christ to become less significant in our lives.

Thirteen Reasons I Don't Go to Sporting Events Anymore

1. Every time I went, they asked me for money.
2. The people sitting in my row didn't seem very friendly.
3. The seats were very hard.
4. The coach never came to visit me.

5. The referees made a decision I didn't agree with.

6. I was sitting with hypocrites—they only came to see what others were wearing!

7. Some games went into overtime, and I was late getting home.

8. The marching band played some songs I had never heard before.

9. The games are scheduled on my only day to sleep in and run errands.

10. My parents took me to too many games when I was growing up.

11. Since I read a book on sports, I feel that I know more than the coaches anyway.

12. I don't want to take my children because I want them to choose for themselves what sport they like best.

13. I can play sports anywhere, I don't need to go to a stadium.

Do these reasons sound familiar? Have you lost your passion for local church ministry? Are you treating Jesus' bride like a social club or an extra-curricular activity?

When you examine the high value of the local church to the heart of Jesus—it will motivate you. His bride will become one of your highest priorities.

GOD STILL WORKS IN THE LOCAL CHURCH

Annually we host an Open House Sunday at our church. It's always one of the single biggest days of the year for reaching out into our community and reaching souls for the Saviour. These days often require some sacrifices in order to fulfill the mission; however, at the end of the day, the sacrifices always pale in comparison to the spiritual fruit they produce.

In preparing the message for an Open House Sunday several years ago, I prayerfully decided to stay in the prophetic series I had been preaching entitled "Times Are Changing." This decision meant that I would preach from Revelation 17 on "The False Church or the True Christ?" This pointed passage speaks of the false church as the great whore and the mystery of Babylon.

Needless to say, this is not the text that most "church growth gurus" would encourage you to preach from on the single day of the year when the most first-time guests would be sitting in the congregation. Frankly, had God not clearly led me, I doubt that I would have chosen this passage!

Amazingly, as the Holy Spirit worked during this message, dozens of people came under conviction—for the first time realizing that they had been blindly following the secular concepts of pluralism and secularism, which ultimately will one day lead to a false global religion. In the conclusion of the message, I challenged the people to not follow religious tolerance and blending of faiths, but to follow the narrow path of Jesus Christ—the only true Saviour.

During the invitation, many responded and trusted Jesus Christ as their personal Saviour. It was overwhelming to see the aisles filled with lost souls coming to Jesus. And I was reminded all over again—it's not about strategies and studies. It's not about slick service programming and secular growth methods. The church belongs to Jesus—and its growth and health depend fully upon His power and our obedience to Him.

THE CHURCH—THE PILLAR AND GROUND OF TRUTH

> But if I tarry long, that thou mayest know how thou oughtest to behave thyself in the house of God, which is the church of the living God, the pillar and ground of the truth.—1 TIMOTHY 3:15

Think about those words, "the pillar and ground of the truth." That's a weighty responsibility! By God's command, your local church holds the eternal truth of God for a waiting world. The truth was given to the church—and it's our responsibility to become grounded upon that truth, and to hold it up high for a lost world to see.

This sheds a whole new light on why we attend church, why we give, and why we serve with our church family. When this consideration finds its way into your heart, it will truly become a sacred motivation. The bride of Christ will stir your heart and compel you to love Jesus, love the lost, and love one another with a pure heart, fervently.

Have you ever heard the story about the man who became president for a day?

President James Polk spent his last day as president on March 3, 1849, and at midnight, Polk was out of office. But his successor, General Zachary Taylor, a staunch churchgoer, refused to be sworn in on March 4, 1849, because it was a Sunday.

In effect he said, "Going to church is a higher priority than becoming president of the United States." He postponed his inauguration until Monday, March 5. So for one day, US Senator David Atchison of Missouri was president *pro tempore* of the nation.

Can you think of anything more important than becoming president of the United States? Zachary Taylor could—it was going to church.

Hebrews 10:24–25 underscores the high priority of the church in our lives: "And let us consider one another to provoke unto love and to good works: Not forsaking the assembling of ourselves together, as the manner of some is; but exhorting one another: and so much the more, as ye see the day approaching."

God could have chosen to do His work Himself, or He could have sent angels to complete the task. But He has graciously given us the privilege of participating with Him and with our church family. It is Christ who adds to and builds the church, but He has chosen to do so through our faithful witness and local church bodies.

There is nothing on Earth more important, more valuable, or nearer to the heart of Christ than what is unfolding each week through the ministries of faithful, Bible-believing churches.

Let the local church become one of your most sacred motivations!

SACRED MOTIVE #6

The Local Church

Putting the Motive into Practice:

Christ gave His very life for the local church. How can you invest yourself into this precious institution?

Commit yourself to a particular local church. The local church is God's method to reach the world with the Gospel and to nurture Christians through discipleship and Bible teaching. It is impossible to be fully involved in this process—either on the receiving or the giving end—without being committed and faithful to a Bible-teaching, local church. Church membership is not only taught in Scripture; it is an important step of commitment and accountability to God's divine institution.

Set the local church as a determining priority. Christ's love for the local church was so passionate that it was a supreme motivator of His sacrifice. When it comes to determining the regular routines of your life or the defining, direction-setting decisions, give the local church the priority which it deserves and which Christ demonstrated.

Personally invest in your church. Matthew 6:21 affirms, "For where your treasure is, there will your heart be also." Giving your time, finances, energy, prayer, and attention to the local church and its ministries ties your heart to the church. Investing yourself will bring a level of motivation that is heartfelt and energized by the Holy Spirit.

Faithfully engage in the work of the local church. Being part of a church that is accomplishing God's work is a blessing; but being personally engaged in God's work is thrilling! Join with your church family in the frontline ministries of evangelism and discipleship. Witness to the lost, support the teaching of God's Word, and pour your life into hands-on ministry through the local church.

THE GENERATIONS FOLLOWING ME

And the things that thou hast heard of me among many witnesses, the same commit thou to faithful men, who shall be able to teach others also.—2 TIMOTHY 2:2

Several times a year I step onto the platform for our Sunday evening church service and welcome a couple of dozen young families onto the platform with me. Each of them is holding a newborn baby for the purpose of dedicating themselves and their child to the Lord. These baby dedications are precious—from the cute antics of the babies to the blessing of seeing a new Christian family grow in God's grace. But perhaps one of the most cherished aspects of these dedications relates to what has transpired over the past decade.

Having served the Lord in the same church for over twenty-five years allows me to dedicate the children of those whom I dedicated in my early years of ministry here. It is a cherished privilege to pray with these second-generation and third-generation Christians—some of whose parents I personally led to Jesus Christ more than two decades ago.

I am thankful that the vast majority of young people who have grown up in our church are still faithful to the Lord today. The biblical foundation they received from Sunday school teachers, youth pastors, and godly mentors has given them stability, maturity, and the ability to follow God's plan for their lives as they begin to raise their children.

As I reflect on the memories of my own children and the young people of our church who are now grown, one truth remains certain in my mind: we never regret the investments we make into the next generation. Whether we make a difference for our own children or for the children in our church and community, the time, prayer, and labor we invest in young lives will reap great dividends as we stay faithful to the Lord.

I am deeply motivated when I see one generation grow into adulthood, begin to live faithfully for the Saviour, and to begin themselves investing in the next generation. It's a sacred thing to understand and accept our responsibility to pass on the baton of faith to those coming behind us.

ME-CENTERED MOTIVES

Culture is constantly compelling us to live for self. Eat, drink, and be merry—seek pleasure, gratify your flesh, and get all you can while you can. The "what happens in Vegas stays in Vegas" mentality has consumed the average American, and it has bent our souls to live with shortsighted motivations. The fact is, what happens in Vegas doesn't stay in Vegas—it ends up on Facebook! And worse yet, it deeply wounds you, leaving scars that remain for the rest of your life.

The flesh is a demanding monster, consuming the soul with lust and the desire for self-serving, immediate gratifications while dismantling long-term values and priorities. Sowing to the flesh brings a harvest of corruption. Although harvest takes time to ripen, it always comes. And when it arrives, oh, how we wish we had planted different seeds.

One of the great costs of the present-day hedonistic lifestyle is the sacrificing of the next generation. Much like the children of Israel in the Old Testament defiled themselves with idolatry and sacrificed their children upon the pagan altar of Molech, today's adults are sacrificing the next generation on the altars of hedonism, fornication, and lasciviousness.

Me-centered motives may bring you instant gratification and allow you to be consumed of your own lusts, but you will not want to reap the harvest that your sin will produce in the lives of those coming behind you.

Truly, one of the most compelling reasons to be faithful to Jesus is that young eyes are watching us. Young hearts are examining us. Future generations are building their lives on the foundations we are laying for them.

Every day of my life I am deeply motivated by seeing young people—elementary kids, teenagers, college students, my own children and grandchildren—as they come behind me. I long to pass on my faith to them and to see them remain faithful and true to their Saviour.

THE GREATEST GENERATION

We often talk about the "greatest generation"—a term coined by the title of Tom Brokaw's book profiling the men and women who served in World War II and helped rebuild America after the Great Depression. Truly, we owe a great debt of gratitude and honor to those who served our country so faithfully—even unto death.

As President Ronald Reagan said, "Freedom is never more than one generation away from extinction. We didn't pass it to our children in the bloodstream. It must be fought for, protected, and handed on for them to do the same, or one day we will spend our sunset years telling our children and our children's children what it was once like in the United States where men were free."

The same could be said of the Christian faith. You can't pass it along in the bloodstream. It doesn't show up in young hearts or lives by osmosis. It must be fought for, intentionally transferred, and deeply implanted into their hearts by faithful Christ-followers who lead the way.

CORE VALUES WE MUST PASS ON

Every Christian should wake up every day determined to intentionally live in a way that mentors the next generation of Christians. This is our calling in Christ. His truth must be handed down to those coming behind us, and this calling is far more sacred than any temporary pleasure or success. For what have we gained if we attain every financial and pleasurable goal only to discover that we have not handed down truth—the faith of Christ?

Consider nine areas—core values—that we must pass on to those coming behind us. These are values we have tried to pass along in our local church as well as on the campus of West Coast Baptist College. May you allow these priorities to weigh heavily in your decisions as you lead those under your influence.

We must uplift sound doctrine.

For if the trumpet give an uncertain sound, who shall prepare himself to the battle?—1 CORINTHIANS 14:8

We must be committed to rightly dividing the Word of Truth through biblical preaching and teaching—giving strong doctrinal content in a fashion that is clear and practical. May we resist current trends to diminish doctrine in order to make the truth palatable to the unregenerate man. Second Corinthians 4:5 emphasizes this need: "For we preach not ourselves, but Christ Jesus the Lord; and ourselves your servants for Jesus' sake."

We must model Christian teamwork.

> Only let your conversation be as it becometh the gospel of Christ: that whether I come and see you, or else be absent, I may hear of your affairs, that ye stand fast in one spirit, with one mind striving together for the faith of the gospel.—PHILIPPIANS 1:27

It is imperative that we recognize God's desire for us to strive together, with our family and church family for the faith of the Gospel. Young people need to see that the faith is worth striving for, and they need to see us lead the way in holding forth the truth in a spirit of unity.

We must strive for biblical balance in our home and ministry life.

> A false balance is abomination to the LORD: but a just weight is his delight.—PROVERBS 11:1

Imbalanced lives, both in ministry and at home, always lead to tragedy. With Christ at the center, may we allow the Word of

God to produce a proper balance. May we balance grace and truth, rules and relationships, holiness and helpfulness, and doctrine with obedience.

We must maintain sincere approachability.

For a bishop must be blameless, as the steward of God; not selfwilled, not soon angry, not given to wine, no striker, not given to filthy lucre;—TITUS 1:7

Self-willed leadership is limiting and unapproachable. We need a new generation of spiritual mentors who are easily approached and transparent. May we have a heart to know, love, nurture, and humbly lead those coming behind us. May they learn from our struggles as well as our victories. May they see true and humble examples of godliness coupled with humility.

We must model consistent soulwinning and discipleship.

Go ye therefore, and teach all nations, baptizing them in the name of the Father, and of the Son, and of the Holy Ghost: Teaching them to observe all things whatsoever I have commanded you: and, lo, I am with you alway, even unto the end of the world. Amen.—MATTHEW 28:19-20

Soulwinning is not only to be "taught," but it must also be "caught" as leadership provides the example in faithfulness. May it be our prayer that, through our leadership, God will raise up a generation of young soulwinners who will be genuinely motivated by the Holy Spirit as He develops a disposition of compassion and faithfulness within their hearts for the Saviour.

We must cultivate hearts for God.

My heart is fixed, O God, my heart is fixed: I will sing and give praise.—PSALM 57:7

The primary goal for our young people reaches far deeper than mere outward conformity. I appreciate young people who obey and honor their authorities, yet mere obedience does not lead to a spiritual heart. May it be our desire to cultivate hearts that hunger for God. May we pray that our young people will passionately and personally pursue Christ and completely yield their hearts to the Lord Jesus. Only then will the next generation walk with the Lord and live for Him their entire lives.

We must model Christian living.

Those things, which ye have both learned, and received, and heard, and seen in me, do: and the God of peace shall be with you.—PHILIPPIANS 4:9

May those coming behind us see genuine Christianity in our lives, and may they receive mentoring in sincere service for the Lord. May the next generation not only hear God's truth, but may they also see it lived out before them.

We must lovingly lead our families.

One that ruleth well his own house, having his children in subjection with all gravity; (For if a man know not how to rule his own house, how shall he take care of the church of God?)—1 Timothy 3:4–5

Husbands, love your wives, even as Christ also loved the church, and gave himself for it.—Ephesians 5:25

God desires for every Christian family to be spiritually healthy and vibrant, and every young person deserves to see and experience a biblical home built upon Christ and living out His love and grace.

We must walk in the Spirit.

But the fruit of the Spirit is love, joy, peace, longsuffering, gentleness, goodness, faith, Meekness, temperance: against such there is no law. And they that are Christ's have crucified the flesh with the affections and lusts. If we live in the Spirit, let us also walk in the Spirit. —Galatians 5:22–25

We cannot, by ourselves, produce the fruit that evidences mature Christianity. Each of us must yield to the Holy Spirit. The Christian life is a holy life. As we endeavor to take the "high road" in the Christian life, we will only find true success in the power and leadership of the Holy Spirit. We must be dead to self to be filled with God's Holy Spirit.

May we raise up a new generation who will know what it means to walk in the Spirit and die to self. May they learn from us to yield to God's Holy Spirit each and every day. And may they be dissatisfied with anything less than Spirit-filled living and Spirit-empowered ministry.

TAKE THE LONG VIEW

Purposefully implanting these core values in the next generation requires diligence, sacrifice, persistence, and faith. Much of the investment we make into young people only bears fruit years after the initial seeds are sown. Too often I have seen parents and youth workers begin well, but then grow weary of the effort and lose their motivation to pass on the faith just before the fruit of their labors would have matured.

One of the most faith-filled decisions that our church ever made was to start West Coast Baptist College. From its beginning, the college surpassed all of our resources in every way—time, money, facilities—everything! To this day, overseeing and caring for the college is a daily walk of faith. Not only that, but it is a lot of work!

Over the years, God has brought together a team of staff and faculty who tirelessly give of themselves to this work of training laborers for His harvest. Even as we pour our lives and our hearts into our students, we do it with gratefulness to have a part in their future labors.

But recently all of these sacrifices came clearly into view when I stepped into a room where some of our alumni had gathered for a luncheon. I was overwhelmed by what I saw—hundreds of men and women who are literally serving the Lord all around the world as pastors, missionaries, assistants, Christian school teachers—faithful servants of God. Seeing so many at the same time astounded me as I realized the magnitude of what God has done through the past years of faith and labor. It was as if God pulled back a curtain and gave me a moment to glimpse a portion of what He has produced through West Coast Baptist College.

God is gracious to give any of us influence into future generations. And He is kind to allow us moments when we see the fruit that He is producing through us as we serve by His grace. These moments remind us to continue teaching, loving, modeling, mentoring, serving, training, counseling—investing into the next generation.

But even during the times that we don't see the fruit of our labor, we must choose to see it with the eyes of faith. We must take the long view, focusing our sights forward to the time when the generation following us will be living the values we have implanted in them and themselves investing in those following them.

THE EYES OF MANASSEH

One of the greatest Bible preachers I have ever called my friend was Evangelist Wally Davis, who went home to Heaven some years ago. Brother Davis preached often for us at church and camp events, and God greatly used him in our lives.

Toward the end of his long battle with cancer, we invited him to preach on a Sunday night to our church family. Although we were praying for God's healing, we suspected that God may take him to Heaven, and we all knew that this could be his last time to preach at Lancaster Baptist Church.

It was a special evening. We decorated the church auditorium as an outdoor area similar to where Brother Davis preached at our annual Men and Boys Campout. We even brought the large tree-stump pulpit from the High Sierras to our platform for the evening.

As Brother Davis stood to preach that night, his large frame was thinner and weaker than usual, but his thundering, preaching voice was still strong and passionate. I'm sure our church family will never forget that night as he preached perhaps his most well-known and God-anointed message, "The Eyes of Manasseh Are Upon You."

He recounted the reign of King Hezekiah—a king of Judah who honored the Lord and under whose leadership the kingdom prospered. But through all of his prosperity and success, Hezekiah sent inconsistent and conflicting signals to his young son. For all the good that he did, he forgot the young eyes of his boy that were watching him, and he failed to pass along his faith. God's Word recounts that after Hezekiah's death, his son, Manasseh, began to reign when he was just twelve years old. And he did evil—even to the point of leading the nation back into idolatry and sacrificing his own children on pagan altars. (You can read the story in 2 Kings 20 and 2 Chronicles 30–31.)

How easy it is to be motivated by earthly success—by money, status, career advancement, and personal pleasure. How easy it is, amidst our busyness and insatiable thirst for more, to forget that the eyes of Manasseh are upon us. The next generation is watching us— examining our faith, testing our lives, and determining whether or not our God is true.

When you are tempted to quit or despair—when you are considering sin or idolatry—remember the eyes of Manasseh. The generations coming behind you are looking at your example. Let this sacred motivation compel you to remain faithful to the Lord and to His truth.

Your faithfulness is the anchor of their faith!

SACRED MOTIVE #7
The Generations Following Me

Putting the Motive into Practice:

Passing your faith to the next generation will never happen by accident. Below are some suggestions to help you intentionally apply the truths of this chapter as you pass the baton of faith to those following you.

Ask the Lord to search your heart for me-centered motives. The pull of the world, the flesh, and the devil is not only strong; sometimes it becomes so common that we don't even notice it. Ask the Holy Spirit to take a thorough spiritual inventory of your heart and point out any seeds of the flesh that you are currently sowing. It is far better to uproot those seeds now than to see a harvest of weeds sprouting in the generation following you.

Purposefully instill core values. Slowly reread the list of core values that we need to pass to succeeding generations, and ask yourself which ones you are actively engaged in passing on. Perhaps giving yourself a letter grade on each would help you see which two or three values you most need to give attention to—first, by modeling them in your own life, and then in mentoring young people.

Visualize the future. All of us encounter seasons of weariness. But there is something about looking ten or twenty years ahead and visualizing the fruit of our investments to reenergize our efforts. Remember that any investment you make in a young heart may not bear fruit today, but it will bear fruit!

MY FAMILY

Train up a child in the way he should go: and when he is old, he will not depart from it.—PROVERBS 22:6

I have no greater joy than to hear that my children walk in truth.—3 JOHN 4

Dear Dad,

You are the kind of dad every girl dreams of. I thank the Lord all the time for placing me in our family...Thank you for raising me in a Christian home...in a godly and balanced environment. Thank you for staying in one place my whole life and for providing consistency and security in our home. Thank you for being such a great leader. Thank you for staying faithful to mom and our family. Thank you for staying faithful

to the Lord. Thank you for being the world's greatest pastor...
for providing godly influences and hundreds of opportunities
to make decisions for the Lord and to grow spiritually in
one place. Thank you for ensuring that we received a quality
education. Thank you for starting a Bible college. Thank you
for the spiritual battles you fight for our family. Thank you for
all the long talks—helping us with bad attitudes or bad grades
or bad friends.

Thank you recently for all the long talks about dating
and the future. Thank you for incredible family vacations and
for the thousands of wonderful memories we share. Dad, you
are the best. God has blessed me beyond measure by allowing
me to grow up in your home. I love you and thank you for all
you've done for me.

Thank you for all the counsel and time you've given
me in my relationship with Peter. Thank you for loving and
guiding me through this transition in my life and for being
patient as I have struggled at times in my communication to
you regarding Peter.

After much prayer, Bible reading, and meditating on
counsel from you and Mom, I believe God has given me
a perfect peace that Peter is the one for me. God has given
me a peace that my heart is not dividing love between you
and Peter...but enlarging my heart to be able to love you
both differently.

Because the Lord has given me such an awesome and
secure upbringing, I have struggled in the aspect of trusting
the Lord in my relationship with Peter in one area: I'm leaving

the known for the unknown. But I do want to enter the unknown with Peter. I don't know what God will have in store for our future, but I am trusting the Lord and am excited to see what He will do with our lives.

I love Peter because he loves the Lord. He has a desire to serve Him. He has a drive to be the best he can be for God. He is patient with me, yet firm when he needs to be. He loves me and is incredibly good to me. He has a consistent spirit and temperament, and he has a good attitude.

I love Peter because of his desire to grow...personally and spiritually. He seeks counsel and lives life on purpose. He makes decisions based on principle, not on whim or preference. I believe that our strengths and weaknesses compliment each other and make us more effective in the Lord's work. He's the first person I want to share things with and my favorite person to be with. He's got the chemistry, competency, and character you've always told me to look for.

Dad, my desire is to live my life in a way that would please the Lord and make you proud. I love you so much...

Love,
Danielle

The letter above was given to me by my oldest daughter some months before she was engaged to our son-in-law, Peter. (I think she was trying to help me through the transition of watching her fall in love!) As you might guess, this letter, and other similar notes from our three other children, are treasures to me.

In God's grace, He has blessed us with four wonderful children who are all married and serving the Lord in ministry. We now have two grandchildren as well. I am so thankful to God for my family, and I want my children and grandchildren to see me faithful to the end.

Somewhere in our society there has developed a disconnection between generations of families. Perhaps this is due to sin and disappointment of various kinds. But all too often, it is due to a lack of motivation on the part of parents and grandparents to purposefully and lovingly lead their families in the ways of the Lord.

I truly believe it is my great privilege and responsibility to continue encouraging our family in the coming years. I want to live in such a way that they will be proud to say "that's my dad/papa." And I want them to be able to look at my life and say, "He was a faithful man of God." I don't ever want to disappoint them.

A WASTE OR AN INVESTMENT

Charles Francis Adams, the grandson of President John Adams, was heavily involved in politics like his grandfather. A congressman, ambassador, and lawyer, his days were full and his schedule demanding. Adams rigorously kept a diary, and he instructed his children to do the same.

One day, Adams recorded, "Went fishing with my son today—a day wasted."

Adams' son, Brooke, also wrote in his journal that day. His entry reads, "Went fishing with my father today—the most wonderful day of my life."

Time spent with our children is an investment—not a waste. Too often we sacrifice our children on pagan altars. We invest our lives into career advancement, ministry needs, and personal pursuits—to the neglect of our family. This idolatrous priority structure brings with it a terrible cost.

But it doesn't have to be that way. One of the greatest motivators in my life is to think of my children and grandchildren. In a day when so many children choose to reject Christ because of parental example, I pray that my family would choose to live for Christ because of my example.

Our family has grown up much too quickly. It seems I am understanding more and more the words of pastors gone before me who have said, "Make your family your first priority in ministry." Although I look back and see times when I could have done much better, I am thankful for every minute I have spent with my children and now with my grandchildren.

Spend time with your family. Make memories together. I'm grateful for a wise wife who, through busy seasons of ministry, often reminded me to do this through the years. Not all of life needs to be lived at the church, and there's nothing unspiritual about relaxing together and enjoying one another.

WHY DISNEYLAND IS GOOD FOR PASTORS AND GRANDFATHERS

My friend, Pastor Dave Teis, has pastored for more than thirty-five years in Las Vegas, Nevada. What I most respect about Pastor Teis is the fact that all of his grown children are walking in the truth and serving in our Lord's work, despite being raised in "Sin City." This, of course, is due to godly upbringing, family devotions, and consistent parenting. But I believe there is another reason his family turned out well: Pastor Teis knows how to have fun with his family.

Often, through his years of pastoring, Brother Teis has taken his family out of Sin City and down to Mickey's Town for a day or two of family fun. (Rumor has it that there is even a paver in the Teis family name at the entry to the Park.)

Our family recently had a great day with our children and two grandchildren at Disneyland. (We arrived as the Teises were heading back to Vegas.) As we enjoyed a day at the park with our grown children and their small children, I couldn't help but consider some ways that Disneyland is helpful for the family—especially families busy in full-time ministry.

1. It's good to have fun with family. Sometimes we all take life and ourselves too seriously.

2. It's great to see a child laugh! "A merry heart doeth good like a medicine" (Proverbs 17:22).

3. Every wife and grandmother appreciates making family memories. And through the years these become cherished reflections.

4. It's a great place for fellowship. I always see Christian friends there. (On this particular trip we visited with our missionaries to El Salvador, the Charters family.)

5. It's a great place to witness. There are plenty of unsaved people at Disneyland, and people accept a friendly Gospel brochure there as well as they do anywhere else.

6. Buzz Lightyear never criticizes me, and Goofy reminds me of _____ (you can fill that in!).

7. The sunshine is helpful in providing Vitamin D. It's refreshing to spend the day outdoors.

I suppose the list could go on. The simple point is, it's healthy—spiritually, emotionally, relationally, and physically—to disconnect at times and spend a day with your family. It's wise to maintain your family relationships in such a way that allows you to have fun, laugh, and enjoy one another along with other good gifts from your Heavenly Father.

GETTING THE PRIORITIES RIGHT

In light of this sacred motivation, allow me to challenge you to live with biblical priorities. Set your life agenda by the will and Word of God in these critical ways:

Make marriage your first ministry.

Your first human commitment is to your spouse. The pace and demands of the Christian life and ministry can add a unique dimension to marriage. But a strong marriage is essential. As the church is Christ's bride, your wife is your bride; and you are the only one who can care for her needs.

Pray for and invest into your children.

Pray for your children. Earnestly. Regularly. Specifically.

Pray with them and for them. Let them know you are praying for them.

Give them time. Deliberately, intentionally, and proactively schedule time to be with, to enjoy, to train, and to fellowship with your children.

Serve the Lord with your family.

Family life and church life—or ministry life—are not incompatible. They should be synergistic. One should complement and complete the other. Your church should benefit because of your strong family, and your family should benefit because of your involvement in a strong church.

One of the greatest ways to invest and spend time together as a family is by serving God together. Perhaps you would partner with your child in reaching a soul for Christ or making a visit to someone enduring a trial. Perhaps you could minister together in some weekend program or ministry. There's no better place to raise up the next generation than around Bible-believing, God-honoring Christian friends and ministry.

Have a family purpose.

Years ago when our kids were elementary age, Terrie and I planned a day to get away to have time to articulate the purpose of our family. After much prayer and Scripture reading, I took out a blank sheet of stationary and wrote these words:

> The mission of our family is to glorify the Lord Jesus Christ through obedience to His written Word, and by edifying and exhorting one another as we grow to understand our diverse yet compatible personalities.

After each of the children had read the new mission statement for our family, we each signed the bottom to pledge our commitment to live in accordance to it. Terrie and I often look back and remember that day as one of our most precious family memories.

Each day as I leave our house, I walk past our written purpose statement. While we are by no means a perfect family, I am thankful that we have done our best to glorify God and edify each other.

Although a written purpose statement is not necessarily a requirement for glorifying God as a family, raising a Christian family to honor God doesn't happen by accident. It takes purpose and commitment.

HOW TO LEAVE A LEGACY FOR YOUR FAMILY

From the moment that Danielle and Peter told us they were expecting our first grandbaby, my perspective shifted in a way you can't understand unless you are a grandparent. Even before little Camden was born, I began planning what kind of legacy I wanted to leave for him. Camden has now been joined by Delanie, our granddaughter, and Terrie and I are thankful for both.

God intends for His truth to pass from one generation to the next. "One generation shall praise thy works to another, and shall declare thy mighty acts" (Psalm 145:4). Whether you are a first-generation Christian or a fifth-generation Christian, you have the privilege and responsibility of passing God's truth to the generation following you.

Live faithfully.

First Corinthians 4:2 says, "Moreover it is required in stewards, that a man be found faithful." Our first responsibility of faithfulness is to God. Will your children and grandchildren remember you as a man or woman who placed God first in every aspect of life?

Our next responsibility is to our families. Our time is short with our children and grandchildren. Let's be faithful to invest in their lives. Our children are watching us. And there is no greater joy than seeing those coming after us walking in truth.

God has also given each Christian a responsibility to the local church. Looking back, I'm so thankful that Terrie and I raised our family in church. I want my grandchildren to one day remember me as a man who was faithful to the church.

Live truly.

Solomon instructed, "Hear, ye children, the instruction of a father, and attend to know understanding. For I give you good doctrine, forsake ye not my law" (Proverbs 4:1–2). Teach your children the truths of God's Word—both theological truths and moral truths. Only God's truth can give them a firm foundation upon which to build their lives. We must leave a legacy for them of embracing true doctrine. Second Timothy 3:15 says, "And that from a child thou hast known the holy scriptures, which are able to make thee wise unto salvation through faith which is in Christ Jesus."

Live liberally.

Leave a legacy of generosity. One of the most generous people I have ever known was my granddad. A hard-working farmer in southwest Colorado, Granddad Chappell gave hundreds of thousands of dollars to the Lord's work over the years. I want to instill a love for generosity in my children and grandchildren. And I want future generations to remember me as a man who gave freely to the Lord, the Lord's people, and my family.

Generosity involves far more than financial resources. We can give our families time, memories, prayers, etc. Invest your life into your children and grandchildren to leave a legacy of generosity.

PILE HIGH THE STONES

As a young boy, I spent hundreds of hours on the tractor with Granddad Chappell. He told me how his dad, my great-granddad, began the farm as a 160-acre homestead in the late 1890s. The soil in southwest Colorado is full of stones, and as we would work through the fields, we'd often come to a large rock. I'd hop off the tractor and place the rock in the scoop kept on the front of the tractor for that purpose. As we'd return to the barn, Granddad would deposit the rocks in a pile of previously collected rocks. There were literally thousands of huge rocks in this pile—all collected one by one over the years.

Today, my uncle and cousins work the Chappell family farm. They drive beautiful tractors equipped with air conditioning, GPS, and stereo. They occasionally find a stone in one of the fields, but thanks to Granddad's diligent labors, most of the stones have already been unearthed and piled out back.

I want my example to do for my children what Granddad's painstaking labors have done for my uncle. Sure, they'll have difficulties of their own, but if I can leave a legacy that will make their road easier, that is a worthwhile investment.

Next to love and loyalty for Christ, the greatest motivators of my life are my wife, children, and grandchildren. I'm motivated by the fact that I want to have something to pass on to my grandchildren.

Every moment of time and sacrifice of energy that we make for our families is an investment worthy of our lives.

SACRED MOTIVE #8
My Family

Putting the Motive into Practice:

Just as the stone pile on the family farm in Colorado was the result of my great-granddad's and granddad's painstaking labors, so piling high the stones for my children and grandchildren will be the result of my purposed choices. What actions can you take to unearth the stones for your family?

Evaluate your priorities. Our priorities are not always reflected in what we *say* is important to us; they are reflected in our daily and weekly schedules. Does your husband or wife know that he or she is your highest priority and that you are committed to a strong, loving marriage? Do your children know that they are more important to you than the hundreds of other demands that pull for your time and attention? Pause to evaluate if your family receives the highest priority in the allotment of your time and energy.

Plan a family time. In our home, I noticed that family time only happened when it was specifically planned and scheduled ahead. Before you move on to the next chapter in this book, schedule a fun, recreational time with your family—perhaps a "family night" this very week, or perhaps a day trip to the zoo. Announce this time to your family, and allow them to enjoy the fun of anticipation.

Look for ways to serve the Lord together. There is nothing like laboring together for the cause of Christ that knits hearts and develops a strong spiritual bond in a family. Find a ministry in your church that you can serve in together—as a family.

Write a family purpose statement. Rally your family around a common and mutually chosen purpose by writing it out and asking all to sign it.

Consider your legacy. One of the greatest investments you can make into the lives of those you love is the personal choices you make to be a faithful, genuine, and generous Christian. Who you are at the core determines the legacy you will leave for others. Ask yourself, "If I were to enter eternity today, what legacy would be left for my family?"

MY COUNTRY'S NEED FOR REVIVAL

Wilt thou not revive us again: that thy people may rejoice in thee?—Psalm 85:6

My country needs revival. America is in sad shape spiritually. Frankly, the whole world is in desperate need of Christ—regardless of the country you call home.

Much of the world is becoming more Islamic and anti-Christian—seemingly overnight. Politically, economically, and spiritually there is an obvious platform taking shape for the coming antichrist and an eventual one-world government and religion.

Tragically, even as our world stands in peril and in desperate need of revival, we are simultaneously witnessing a weakening of convictions and a loss of spiritual fervor among Christians in many nations. Christendom is growing increasingly lukewarm and unstable theologically—especially in America, where Christians have been most blessed.

As the world is increasingly ripe for the fulfillment of end-times prophecy, so are the hearts of men ripe for the Gospel and an end-times harvest of souls. The darker the night, the brighter the light. And one great motivator to live for Christ is the desperate need for revival amongst God's people—both in America and around the world.

TRUE PATRIOTISM

I've never been more thankful to be an American. I'm thankful for the men who pledged their "lives, fortunes, and sacred honor" to sign the Declaration of Independence and then gave of themselves in unspeakable sacrifice to birth this great nation.

These men understood that patriotism meant so much more than grabbing the family rifle and charging the redcoats. It involved giving whatever was necessary to uphold the God-given values of freedom and equality which they had come to embrace. For many, patriotism meant giving their lives, their families, and their fortunes. They purchased freedom at a heavy personal expense.

I'm thankful for the heritage of these patriots, statesmen, and soldiers who embraced and upheld freedom—even at the expense of themselves.

I'm thankful for men and women around the world today (some from our church family) who are sacrificing for continued freedom.

But more than the patriotism of a soldier, we need another kind of patriotism today. America is in a state of spiritual and moral decline that is frightening. We seem to have lost our moral compass and our willingness to sacrifice for the biblical values of truth and righteousness.

Today, we need the kind of patriotism that Nehemiah of old embraced. Nehemiah's nation was in desperate straits. The wall of Jerusalem was burned and broken down, and the enemies of the Lord mocked the city's disgrace.

But when Nehemiah heard of the travail of Jerusalem, he made a decision to give his life to the cause of revival. This is what we need today—godly men and women who, motivated by the need for revival, will wholly give themselves to the ministry.

I really believe that the answer to our country's need is not in government reform, but in the spreading of the Gospel of Christ through the ministry of the local church.

How specifically did Nehemiah give his life to see his nation revived? In the coming pages we will examine how the need for revival motivated Nehemiah to action. May the traits present in Nehemiah's life be present in our lives as well, and may each of us live with the compelling motivation to see God bring revival to our land.

MOTIVATED TO FERVENT PRAYER

To Nehemiah, the need was so great that he agonized. He wept and mourned before the Lord. R.A. Torrey observed, "We are too busy to pray, and so we are too busy to have power. We have a great deal of activity but accomplish little. Many services but few results."

When Nehemiah saw the spiritual state of his home, he was moved to fervent prayer. He was motivated to respond spiritually and biblically—and God honored that response. James 5:16 says, "…The effectual fervent prayer of a righteous man availeth much."

Historical precedence points to America's Christian heritage in which many of our political leaders recognized our need for God and sought His help through prayer. Throughout our history, even in recent years, our leaders have offered public prayers seeking the hand of God's blessing.

> "It cannot be emphasized too clearly and too often that this nation was founded, not by religionists, but by Christians; not on religion, but on the Gospel of Jesus Christ. For this very reason, peoples of other faiths have been afforded asylum, prosperity, and freedom of worship here." Patrick Henry, in a speech to the House of Burgesses, May of 1765.

> "God governs in the affairs of man. And if a sparrow cannot fall to the ground without His notice, is it probable that an empire can rise without His aid?" Benjamin Franklin, addressing the Constitutional Convention of 1787.

"I have a tender reliance on the mercy of the Almighty, through the merits of the Lord Jesus Christ. I am a sinner. I look to Him for mercy; pray for me." Alexander Hamilton, upon his death bed, July 12, 1804.

"Almighty God: Our sons, pride of our nation, this day have set upon a mighty endeavor, a struggle to preserve our Republic, our religion and our civilization, and to set free a suffering humanity....Lead them straight and true; give strength to their arms, stoutness to their hearts, steadfastness in their faith. They will need Thy blessings." Franklin D. Roosevelt, in an address to the American people, D-day, June 6, 1944.

"May we be willing to stop our feverish activities and listen to what Thou hast to say, that our prayers shall not be the sending of night letters, but conversations with God. This we ask in Jesus' name. Amen." Peter Marshall, Chaplain of the US Senate, in the opening prayer for Congress, June 27, 1947.

"To preserve our blessed land we must look to God....It is time to realize that we need God more than He needs us....We also have His promise that we could take to heart with regard to our country, that 'If my people, which are called by my name shall humble themselves, and pray and seek my face, and turn from their wicked ways; then will I hear from heaven and will forgive their sin, and will heal their land.'" Ronald Reagan, in a speech given on February 6, 1986.

"May we strive to be of one heart and mind as we seek to accomplish Your divine purpose, here on earth as it is in

Heaven. We ask all of this in the name of our Lord and Saviour Jesus Christ. Amen." Vaughn Baker, in the opening prayer for Congress, October 7, 2009.

Revisionists of American history are diligently seeking to erase our Christian heritage and deny the right to public prayers. This is not merely an issue concerning the separation of church and state—it is an attempt to remove God from the hearts and minds of our citizens.

Yet, I believe it possible for our nation to return to her heritage of prayer. God says, "If my people, which are called by my name, shall humble themselves, and pray, and seek my face, and turn from their wicked ways; then will I hear from heaven, and will forgive their sin, and will heal their land" (2 Chronicles 7:14).

We can complain about the godless trends of our day (and certainly we should use every resource available to change them), but when was the last time you cried out to God to heal our land? Why fight for prayer in public if we do not pray in private?

MOTIVATED TO LIVE WITH PURITY

One of the first things Nehemiah did was acknowledge and confess sin. He expressed a repentant heart toward the sins of his nation. Even so, the need for national revival points us to keep our own hearts right with God and our homes and ministries fervent for Him.

Proverbs 28:13 teaches us, "He that covereth his sins shall not prosper, but whoso confesseth and forsaketh them shall have mercy."

Ephesians 4:30–32 instructs, "And grieve not the holy Spirit of God, whereby ye are sealed unto the day of redemption. Let all bitterness, and wrath, and anger, and clamour, and evil speaking, be put away from you, with all malice: And be ye kind one to another, tenderhearted, forgiving one another, even as God for Christ's sake hath forgiven you."

Spiritual backsliding (to which we are all prone) involves a process of rationalization and lethargy that masks our trend away from God and rationalizes our sin. Carnality disguises itself in spiritual apathy—both nationally and personally. Often, we do not experience revival because we are in love with our sin more than we are in love with Christ. Proverbs 21:2 reminds us, "Every way of a man is right in his own eyes: but the LORD pondereth the hearts."

When revival comes, our love for God reignites and brings with it a greater repulsion toward sin. In God's process of revival, this love is growing brighter and hotter. Revival should not merely be a moment in time, but rather the constant norm of a Christian growing in God's grace.

Growing up, I had some memorable incidents with go-karts. It was always a lot of fun to race them around with friends and pretend to be a "grown-up" with my own car. All of the go-karts I drove fit into one of two categories. The first category were those with inhibitors (or governors), a mechanical device that—for obvious safety reasons—would limit the flow of fuel into the engine, and therefore keep the go-kart from traveling at its maximum potential speed. The second category had no such mechanical restrictions. The flow of fuel was fully open, and the go-kart would travel as fast as the small engine would carry it. While the first type might have been more safe and sensible, you might guess which type I enjoyed driving most.

Too many believers are living their Christian lives with limiters constantly restricting the flow of God's grace and power; they are not reaching the full potential of the purpose and plan that God has for their lives. These limiters can be wrong attitudes, wrong influences, or hidden sin.

I challenge you to look into your life and ask the Holy Spirit to help you discern the inhibitors in your life that keep you from reaching your full potential and usefulness for God. Confess and forsake them, and start living your Christian life with the fuel line of God's empowering grace wide open!

MOTIVATED TO ENGAGE IN MINISTRY

Nehemiah did not just have an idealistic burden; he was personally involved. He helped to build the walls with his own hands. His burden led him to service.

I believe Nehemiah's purpose statement can be found in Nehemiah 2:10: "…to seek the welfare of the children of Israel." This man was motivated by the need for revival—and that motivation moved him to action in serving and leading. Nehemiah's primary concern was the people's spiritual welfare, followed by their physical welfare. He didn't journey to Jerusalem to pass out food stamps or birth control; he desired for his nation to return to God and restore their relationship with Him.

Even so, the greatest need of our land is not better government or more effective social programs. More than anything else we need more obedient churches. We need Christians who will personally and faithfully engage in local church ministry.

MOTIVATED TO ENDURE

Nehemiah faced ridicule, criticism, discouragement, temptation, false accusation, and compromise. Yet he persisted—he faithfully endured to fulfill the call of God. His motivation for national revival trumped all setbacks. It was more powerful than any form of resistance.

While others pressed Nehemiah to compromise and give in, he declared, "…I am doing a great work, so that I cannot come down: why should the work cease, whilst I leave it, and come down to you?" (Nehemiah 6:3). He refused to let trials and resistance derail his cause for God.

The Apostle Paul felt the same way. In 2 Corinthians 4:1 he said, "Therefore seeing we have this ministry, as we have received mercy, we faint not." Again in verses 8–10 of the same chapter he said, "We are troubled on every side, yet not distressed; we are perplexed, but not in despair; Persecuted, but not forsaken; cast down, but not destroyed; Always bearing about in the body the dying of the Lord Jesus, that the life also of Jesus might be made manifest in our body."

MOTIVATED TO SACRIFICE

We need more patriots like Nehemiah. He prayed with compassion and fervency. And he made it his purpose to seek the spiritual welfare of the city. He persevered through criticism, attacks, and discouragement. And in the end, he did what his enemies said couldn't be done—he revived the stones to build a great wall around the city.

This kind of revival and spiritual leadership requires great personal sacrifice. Revival does not come accidentally, nor will it come arbitrarily. It comes as God's people live sacrificially in seeking His face, repenting of sin, and giving themselves to His call.

I love my country and still believe it's the greatest nation on Earth. But sadly, America has steadily drifted away from the founding biblical principles that have made her so great. Today, she is in desperate need of revival.

As political candidates look to reforms, propositions, and parties to offer change and hope, we must realize that our nation's spiritual needs are much deeper than her economic and political needs. Recently, Mr. Barack Obama became the first sitting president to advocate same-sex marriage. Politicians will do many things to please their "base," but godly Christians seek to please God. We must not forget that the Creator who has given rights has also given laws.

America's greatest need is Jesus. And God has called you and me to make a difference. He has called us to be salt and light in this difficult hour. Your spiritual influence is needed.

It's not difficult to be motivated to spiritual service and faithfulness when you see the needs of our nation. If you find yourself lacking in motivation, just look around you. See the spiritual destitution of people. See the spiritual desperation of our nation. Let these needs motivate you to continue living for Christ and sharing His truth with others.

> If my people, which are called by my name, shall humble themselves, and pray, and seek my face, and turn from their wicked ways; then will I hear from heaven, and will forgive their sin, and will heal their land.
> —2 CHRONICLES 7:14

My Country's Need for Revival

Putting the Motive into Practice:

Reading the biblical biography of Nehemiah's life is both inspiring and sobering. It is inspiring because it confirms that even when a nation has reached ruinous spiritual and political lows, God is able to bring revival. It is sobering because it reveals our desperate need for Christians like Nehemiah—true patriots who will be channels through which God will send revival.

As we close this chapter, I encourage you to review the list of Nehemiah's attributes outlined below and ask some soul-searching questions regarding their presence in your life and how you can take steps to grow in these areas:

Motivated to fervent prayer:

- Do I daily spend time in prayer?
- Do I have a prayer list that includes current national needs and the names of those who lead my country?
- Do I regularly and earnestly pray for revival?

Motivated to live with purity:

- Do I keep short accounts with God, regularly seeking His forgiveness when I sin?

- How long has it been since my heart was broken, contrite before God over the sin in my own life?

- Is there an area in my life in which I know I am currently resisting the conviction of the Holy Spirit?

Motivated to engage in ministry:

- In what areas of personal ministry through my local church am I currently involved?

- Am I diligent and faithful to keep my ministry commitments?

- Is there an additional ministry in which the Holy Spirit has been prompting me to engage? What is the first step I need to take to begin?

Motivated to endure:

- What trials or resistance am I currently facing? Or what type of resistance in the past has been most wearisome to me?

- Am I facing a temptation to compromise my faith?

- Which Scripture verses or passages should I memorize and review to strengthen my endurance for Christ?

Motivated to sacrifice:

- Have I made any personal sacrifices for the cause of Christ or for the sake of revival?

- Do I love my God and the people of my nation enough to give myself to prayer and to personally engage in faithfully sharing the Gospel?

- Am I willing to pledge myself to the cause of revival—for a lifetime or until Christ returns?

MY CALLING IN CHRIST

I therefore, the prisoner of the Lord, beseech you that ye walk worthy of the vocation wherewith ye are called, With all lowliness and meekness, with longsuffering, forbearing one another in love; Endeavouring to keep the unity of the Spirit in the bond of peace.—EPHESIANS 4:1–3

One of the greatest memories of my life took place when I was a seventh grader at summer camp in Palmer Lake, Colorado. During the Friday night service, my father preached the Word of God, and the Holy Spirit spoke to my heart, unmistakably calling me to preach the Gospel.

I don't regret my surrender during that defining moment of my life. I will be eternally thankful that God gave me the privilege to serve

Him with a purpose. Like Paul, I can say, "And I thank Christ Jesus our Lord, who hath enabled me, for that he counted me faithful, putting me into the ministry" (1 Timothy 1:12). Remembering the purpose God gave me motivates me to walk worthy of this vocation.

It is obvious, when you study the life of the Apostle Paul, that there were two great motivating factors in his life.

First—Paul never got over the fact that the Son of God had personally died for his sin. As we saw in chapter five, the love of Christ motivated Paul like perhaps no other motivation in his life. In 2 Corinthians 5:14–15 he wrote, "For the love of Christ constraineth us; because we thus judge, that if one died for all, then were all dead: And that he died for all, that they which live should not henceforth live unto themselves, but unto him which died for them, and rose again."

An understanding of God's love and grace had not caused Paul to live carelessly; it had, in fact, increased his devotion. Christ's love compelled him to holiness and passionate ministry.

Second—Paul never got over the fact that the Lord Jesus had personally given to him the ministry of reconciliation. Again, in 2 Corinthians 5, he wrote, "And all things are of God, who hath reconciled us to himself by Jesus Christ, and hath given to us the ministry of reconciliation" (2 Corinthians 5:18). After his salvation, Paul never forgot that God gave him a new purpose for living.

Sadly, we live in a day when most Christians accept God's gift of salvation and hardly return to thank Him for it, much less begin to understand their call to Christ. Many Christians never discover the new purpose and high calling to which they were called at the moment they trusted Christ.

Many never move beyond spiritual infancy. They never discover growth in grace, spiritual maturity, and the sacred call of the Gospel. I'm not saying that everyone is called to full-time vocational ministry. But God's Word is clear that every Christian is called to Christ, to the ministry of reconciliation, and to a consecrated life of service to the Saviour. The fact that you may or may not be called to full-time ministry does not negate your call to full-time Christianity. This call is upon every believer.

I once read the story of the little girl who was frustrated because she didn't have enough important things to carry with her. She had watched her mother and grandmother and had studied what they carried in their purses—the money, the credit cards, the identification, and all the other countless important things that reside in a woman's purse. And she was discouraged.

So, she decided to dig her birth certificate out of the family filing cabinet. She placed it in her purse and carried it to school, feeling confident that she finally had something important in her possession.

Later that day, while outside during recess at school, she pulled out her birth certificate to show some friends. At that moment, a gust of wind blew by, ripping the valuable document from her grasp and whisking it over the fence and away. It was gone. Her friends laughed and left her. And she sat down and began to cry.

A few minutes later, the janitor walked by and asked her what was wrong. With tear-filled eyes, she said, "I just lost my excuse for being born."

Honestly, a lot of Christians and a lot of churches seem to have lost their excuse for being born. They have forgotten their high calling in Christ Jesus. They have lost sight of the fact that they are a peculiar people, a royal priesthood, a chosen generation—redeemed by the blood of Jesus and set apart for His cause and His pleasure. They have become trapped in the world's mindset of survival, materialism, and hedonism—and these things have left them empty and unmotivated.

If you are in Christ, you have a holy calling—an eternal purpose given to you in Christ Jesus before the world began. As you read the verses below, notice the emphasis that Scripture places on our calling in Christ.

> Blessed be the God and Father of our Lord Jesus Christ, who hath blessed us with all spiritual blessings in heavenly places in Christ: According as he hath chosen us in him before the foundation of the world, that we should be holy and without blame before him in love:
> —Ephesians 1:3–4

Wherefore the rather, brethren, give diligence to make your calling and election sure: for if ye do these things, ye shall never fall:—2 PETER 1:10

Who hath saved us, and called us with an holy calling, not according to our works, but according to his own purpose and grace, which was given us in Christ Jesus before the world began,—2 TIMOTHY 1:9

CALLED TO THE GOSPEL

First and foremost, as a Christian, you are called to the Gospel—to share the message of salvation with others. The Christian life and ministry is all about proclaiming the Gospel.

First Thessalonians 2:4–6 teaches, "But as we were allowed of God to be put in trust with the gospel, even so we speak; not as pleasing men, but God, which trieth our hearts. For neither at any time used we flattering words, as ye know, nor a cloke of covetousness; God is witness: Nor of men sought we glory, neither of you, nor yet of others, when we might have been burdensome, as the apostles of Christ."

Paul saw the Gospel as a valuable treasure committed to his trust—a treasure that he was responsible to deliver to others. The sacredness of this calling held him to a standard of purity, transparency, honesty, and grace. The urgency of this calling compelled him to passionate service—to invest every resource of his life into delivering the Gospel which had been committed to his trust.

CALLED TO GROWTH

Second, every Christian is called to grow in grace—to enter the full-time process of personal transformation by the Holy Spirit of God. Second Peter 3:18 instructs, "But grow in grace, and in the knowledge of our Lord and Saviour Jesus Christ. To him be glory both now and for ever. Amen."

From the moment we trust Christ as our Saviour, we are called to be conformed to the image of Christ. God Himself oversees this process (Romans 8:28–30), but He instructs us to yield to the Holy Spirit of God as He works to transform us from the inside out (Romans 12:1–2).

The obstacles to or absence of spiritual growth in our lives always have more to do with our own hearts than with our circumstances or environments. God can turn the most adverse circumstances into stepping stones for our growth, but we must be committed to choosing to yield to Him and purposefully seek to grow in grace.

CALLED TO FAITHFULNESS

Third, every Christian is called to a faithful life. First Corinthians 4:2 highlights the priority of faithfulness: "Moreover it is required in stewards, that a man be found faithful."

As stewards of the Gospel and ambassadors of God's grace, perhaps no quality is of greater importance than our faithfulness. In fact, when we stand before the Lord to give an account of how we have stewarded our calling, the quality that He will most praise is faithfulness: "Well done, thou good and faithful servant: thou hast been faithful over a few things, I will make thee ruler over many things: enter thou into the joy of thy lord" (Matthew 25:21).

Perhaps you have seen Christians who have lived with only a sporadic understanding of the calling of God in their lives. For intermittent seasons, they will commit themselves to fulfill the call of sharing the Gospel and to personal growth in God's grace. But their motivation is only an off-and-on decision—not a steady commitment. It is the calling of faithfulness that compels us to not only share the Gospel and to grow in grace, but to do it with persistent consistency—and to do it for a lifetime.

THE CALL OF GOD IS A SACRED PRIVILEGE

Consider the profound privilege and the sacred responsibility it is to be "called of God." Even as you chose Him at salvation, so He has chosen you to labor with Him—to carry out His purpose through your life. The eternal, almighty God of the universe invites you to enter into a timeless investment with your time. Your brief, vapor-like existence on this planet has eternal implications and divine significance. You are on a mission with the Saviour of all mankind. You are His vessel, His instrument, His ambassador.

Are you ignoring your calling for personal pursuits? Have you lost sight of the significance of your days? Have you forgotten your value to the heart and plan of God?

Circumstances will discourage you. People will disappoint you. Emotions will lie to you. Relationships will mislead you. Imagination will deceive you. Life will mistreat you. Human strength will fail you. But God has anointed you for a high calling that rises above all of these things. His calling is constant. In His will, fulfilling His purpose, you will know the greatest success that any human being could ever know—the accomplishment of your God-given mission on planet earth.

Are you looking for motivation to press on? Consider God's call on your life. As long as your heart is beating, He has a calling for you to accomplish. Embrace the joy, the hope, the blessed life of living to fulfill the call of God upon you!

> I therefore, the prisoner of the Lord, beseech you that
> ye walk worthy of the vocation wherewith ye are called,
> —EPHESIANS 4:1

That ye might walk worthy of the Lord unto all pleasing, being fruitful in every good work, and increasing in the knowledge of God;—COLOSSIANS 1:10

That ye would walk worthy of God, who hath called you unto his kingdom and glory.—1 THESSALONIANS 2:12

You have a high calling! In light of His call, continue to walk worthy!

SACRED MOTIVE #10

My Calling to Ministry

Putting the Motive into Practice:

God's calling on our lives is that we would live as full-time Christians—committed to living out His purposes for our lives. Just as the most valuable contributors to the secular workforce are committed to ongoing growth in their vocations, so Christians dedicated to the calling of God in their lives will strive for personal growth in accomplishing that calling. Below are four ways that we can strive for growth in fulfilling God's call:

Acknowledge your need to grow. Perhaps the greatest threat to pursuing excellence in any area is a prideful spirit. And perhaps the most refreshing trait of a growing Christian is a humility that acknowledges the need to grow.

Paul expressed this spirit in Philippians 3:12–14: "Not as though I had already attained, either were already perfect: but I follow after, if that I may apprehend that for which also I am apprehended of Christ Jesus. Brethren, I count not myself to have apprehended: but this one thing I do, forgetting those things which are behind, and reaching forth unto those things which are before, I press toward the mark for the prize of the high calling of God in Christ Jesus."

We so easily become comfortable and complacent, but I believe it is refreshing to the Lord when we acknowledge that our thirst for Him, our knowledge of His Word, our faithfulness in witnessing is not what it could or should be.

Map out a strategy for growth. Acknowledging your need for growth is just the starting point. But we must move beyond that to determine specific actions we can take to grow in our effectiveness as Christian servants.

Ask the Holy Spirit to highlight specific areas of your life that need attention and then to direct you to resources that will help you grow in these areas. Consider if you need to seek out a mentor in soulwinning or to establish accountability for faithfulness. Maybe you need to study out a particular topic in Scripture or read a book on needful areas of Christian growth—marriage, parenting, time management, etc.

I suggest that you actually write out a plan for growth that gives you a systematic approach and involves specific, measurable goals and periodic checkpoints.

Pray for a passion to make a difference. I have often reminded our church staff, "We need a healthy dissatisfaction with the status quo." If you want to see God use you in a greater way, ask Him to put this healthy dissatisfaction in your heart. Specifically pray for the passion the Paul expressed in the verses above. Seek the face of God, and ask Him to give you grace to grow in Him and to live out the calling that He has ordained for your life.

Move forward with courage and obedience as God opens doors for you to fulfill your calling. As surely as you ask the Lord to give you passion to live out your calling, He will open doors of opportunity for you to do so! Walking through these doors will often call you to move outside of your comfort zone and to stretch your faith to act beyond your capabilities. But every time you courageously take a step of obedient faith, the Lord will give you the resources and ability to live out the calling He has placed on your life—a calling greater than you could ever accomplish without His help.

CONCLUSION

Living for God is not only our sacred privilege as Christians, but it is the most fulfilling, rewarding life possible.

Yet sometimes in the midst of our service, we lose sight of why we do what we do. We slip into a pattern of empty routines, forgetting that there is a purpose to our lives—a driving motivation to live for and serve our Lord.

In these pages, we have examined ten motivations—ten compelling reasons to wake up each morning and invest our most wholehearted energy in living for God:

1. **The Glory of God**—God's glory calls us to the highest standard of excellence and is worthy of our greatest devotion.

2. **A Lost World**—A ready harvest of souls surrounds us, and Christ has called us—His laborers—to compassionately reach them with His message of redeeming grace.

3. **My Acceptance in Christ**—Serving out of the joy of knowing that we are already accepted in Christ frees us from the tyranny of our own egos and allows us to serve unhindered in the power of His Spirit.

4. **The Word of God**—In this valuable resource we have everything we need to serve a lifetime of fruitful ministry. God's Word sustains, encourages, corrects, renews, and upholds us.

5. **The Love of Christ**—Christ's love for us is pure, unchanging, and worthy of our highest adoration. Experiencing Christ's love constrains us to joyfully live for His purposes.

6. **The Local Church**—What an honor to be part of the bride of Christ and to with it hold high the truth of the Gospel. The local church is God's program and His means of reaching a lost world.

7. **The Generations Following Me**—Eager hands are waiting for us to pass on the baton of faith, and young eyes are watching our example to know how to carry it.

8. **My Family**—There is no greater joy than to see your children and grandchildren walk in truth. To this end, we invest love, time, training, and prayer into the lives of our families.

9. **My Country's Need for Revival**—The need for true patriotism is greater now than ever before. The sin surrounding us calls us to increase our fervency in prayer and our passion in witnessing for Christ.

10. **My Calling in Christ**—The fact that Christ would entrust to our care His Gospel and that He would call us to a lifetime of growth and faithfulness motivates us to be bold witnesses and to be consistent in our growth.

What could be a stronger stimulant in compelling us to live for God than these sacred motives?

With all my heart, I long to hear Christ Himself say to me, "Well done, thou good and faithful servant..." (Matthew 25:21). As anyone who has ever delegated a project to another knows, "well done" doesn't just refer to *what* we do, but also to *how* we do it. And there is nothing that influences how we serve God like the motives we hold for serving Him.

Do Christians sometimes serve with lower motivations? Yes, I know from experience how easy it is to fall into the traps of serving out of guilt, for man's approval, or for any number of lower causes.

While these motives may initially seem to call forth the same outward actions as sacred motives, they cannot sustain a lifetime of Spirit-filled, fruitful service. Simply put, *why* you do what you do will determine *how long* you do it and how eternally fruitful it will be.

The psalmist understood how vital his motives were. Because he realized that his heart and his thoughts were as important as his actions, he prayed, "Search me, O God, and know my heart: try me, and know my thoughts: And see if there be any wicked way in me, and lead me in the way everlasting" (Psalm 139:23–24). When I have sensed my motives slipping into man-centered or flesh-generated reasons to serve, I have often echoed this prayer. And with it, I claim the confidence that God will indeed reveal any impure motives or fleshly agendas in my heart and lead me in ways of truth.

I encourage you to likewise ask the Lord to search your heart. Are you living from the sacred motives God has given us? Do your actions flow from motives that compel you to worship-filled, love-initiated, Spirit-led, faithful service?

Perhaps you already have experienced serving from these motives, but their fervency in your heart has waned. I pray that these pages have helped to reignite your spirit and realign your perspective.

God is good to allow us to serve Him. And He has every right to call us to serve Him for duty alone. Yet in His grace, He calls us to serve Him from hearts that are focused on His goodness, renewed in His grace, and energized by His purposes.

Serving God is a privilege. Serving Him with the sacred motives He implants in our hearts is a delight!

ABOUT THE AUTHOR

PAUL CHAPPELL is the senior pastor of Lancaster Baptist Church and president of West Coast Baptist College in Lancaster, California. His biblical vision has led the church to become one of the most dynamic Baptist churches in the nation. His preaching is heard on Daily in the Word, a daily radio broadcast heard across America. Pastor Chappell has four children who are married and serving in Christian ministry. He has been married to his wife Terrie for over thirty years.

Connect with Paul Chappell at PaulChappell.com

Visit us online

strivingtogether.com

wcbc.edu

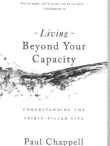